MW01488465

**Other Kaplan Books for 8th Graders**

High School 411

Grammar Power

Learning Power

Reading Power

Math Power

**Other Kaplan Books for the TAAS**

No Stress Guide to the Exit-Level TAAS

Parent's Guide to the TAAS for Grade 3

# Ultimate TAAS*

## Grade 8

**Cynthia and Drew Johnson**

*Texas Assessment of Academic Skills

### Simon & Schuster

NEW YORK · LONDON · SINGAPORE · SYDNEY · TORONTO

Kaplan Publishing
Published by Simon & Schuster
1230 Avenue of the Americas
New York, NY 10020

For bulk sales to schools, please contact: Order Department, Simon & Schuster, 100 Front Street, Riverside, NJ 08075. Phone: 1-800-223-2336. Fax: 1-800-943-9831.

Project Editor: Ruth Baygell
Contributing Editors: Marc Bernstein, Marcy Bullmaster
Cover Design: Cheung Tai
Production Manager: Michael Shevlin
Interior Page Design and Layout: Laurel Douglas
Production Editor: Maude Spekes
Managing Editor: Dave Chipps
Executive Editor: Del Franz

Manufactured in the United States of America

September 2000
10 9 8 7 6 5 4 3 2 1

Library of Congress Cataloging-in-Publication Data is available.

ISBN: 0-7432-0273-2

All of the practice questions in this book were created by the authors to illustrate question types. They are not actual test questions. For information on the TAAS, visit the Texas Department of Education Web site at www.tea.state.tx.us/student.assessment.

# TABLE OF CONTENTS

# ABOUT THE AUTHORS

### Cynthia and Drew Johnson

Cynthia Johnson is the author of several educational books for young people, two of which received the prestigious Parent's Choice Gold Award in 1995, and were listed in *Curriculum Administrator* magazine's "Top 100" educational products for 1996. Drew Johnson is an education writer and editor, creating workbook, textbook, and Web-based education materials for children of all ages. The Johnsons have authored *Kaplan Learning Power*, a guide for improving study skills, and Kaplan's No-Stress Guides and Parent's Guides to various statewide standardized tests.

**KAPLAN**

## HOW TAKING THE GRADE 8 TAAS IS
## SIMILAR TO DRIVING A CAR FOR THE FIRST TIME

You sit down, trying to remember all the things you know you're supposed to remember. The people around you seem to be feeling the same way you do—a little nervous. An adult looks at you and points at his watch, telling you it's time to start. There's no chance of going back now: It's time to take the Grade 8 TAAS.

*Navigating the TAAS can sometimes be a confusing experience.*

© 2000 Picture Quest Inc./© 2000 PhotoSpin Inc.

You're probably familiar with the Texas Assessment of Academic Skills (TAAS) tests already, having taken them throughout your school career. The version you'll take in grade 8 is similar to its grade 7 sibling, but there are a few added sections. Both tests cover mathematics and reading, but the grade 8 test also includes writing, science, and social science. All of these are multiple-choice tests, though the writing section includes an essay.

The grade 8 TAAS isn't just any old test, however. The state ranks 6,600 schools according to test performance, showing how well or how poorly their students fared on the exam. Schools that do well or show marked improvement are rewarded, and schools that do badly face the possibility of having their principal fired, and ceding the school's control to the state. As for the individual eighth grader, a plan is in place to make passing the grade 8 TAAS mandatory for promotion, but this won't occur until 2008. Currently, it's up to each local school district to decide whether you're required to pass the test. In districts where it *is* required, you face the following two equations:

> Equation 1:
> You + good TAAS scores = promotion to the ninth grade

> Equation 2:
> You − good TAAS scores = retake the grade 8 TAAS until
> you achieve a passing score on
> all subjects

To date, the Science and Social Science tests have **not** been used to determine whether you may advance to the next grade. In districts that make passing the grade 8 TAAS mandatory, only the Math, Reading, and Writing tests are relevant.

You don't need to be Albert Einstein to recognize that equation 1 is more desirable than equation 2. Fortunately, if you fail only one subject on the grade 8 TAAS—for example, you pass the Math and Reading TAAS but don't get a high enough score on the Writing exam—you have to take only that one subject test over again. Of course, since most people are not thrilled about standardized tests, this could well be called "finding the silver lining in the cloud." Yet there's no need to feel bad if you do happen to get a low score, because you are not alone. Although TAAS scores have increased in recent years, each year roughly 20,000–40,000 eighth grade students fail at least one of the exams.

The minimum number of questions needed to pass each subject test is defined as follows by the Texas Education Agency (TEA):

*Reading:*       37 out of 48 questions correct

*Math:*       45 out of 60 questions correct

*Writing:*     Essay scores range from 1–4 (highest), and for which a 2 is the minimum passing score. The score you receive on the essay will determine how many multiple-choice questions you'll need to answer correctly.

*Science:*     30 out of 40 questions correct

*Social Studies:*  32 out of 40 questions correct

## How the TAAS Tests Were Born

Currently, there are two different stories circulating about the origin of the TAAS tests.

### Version A:

Ten years ago, on the coldest night of winter, a 100-pound meteor crashed into a field two miles from Enchanted Rock. The meteor cracked open on impact, and at its core were the very first TAAS tests.

### Version B:

In 1990 the state created the TAAS tests in order to establish a statewide system of accountability for Texas schools. The tests were designed to determine how well students were mastering the basic curriculum skills laid out by the TEA. At first, the tests were given only to fourth-, eighth-, and tenth-graders, but in 1993, because of new legislation, all grades from two through eight adopted the test as well. In 1999, Senate Bill 103 mandated that the exit-level test be moved from grade 10 to grade 11, and as of 2003, eleventh graders will be required to pass the TAAS English language arts, mathematics, science, and social studies sections in order to graduate.

© 2000 PhotoSpin Inc.

*While on a stroll, an educator watches a batch of TAAS tests fall to Earth.*

While most people prefer Version B because of its greater adherence to the facts, Version A does have the advantage of making a better made-for-television story.

Whichever story you prefer, the truth is that the TAAS is here to stay, and that's why this book was written. If taking the grade 8 TAAS is like driving a car for the first time, then *Ultimate TAAS* provides you with cool wheels, a great road map, the best insurance, and the training you need to make it a successful experience. You'll find the techniques and strategies needed to do well on each subject test, as well as TAAS-like sample questions to help you practice them. If you study these strategies and apply them on the test, then taking the grade 8 TAAS should change from a difficult experience into something as easy as driving to the beach on the first day of summer break.

If you'll be in the 11th grade in the spring of 2004 or later, you'll be required to pass the English language arts, mathematics, science, and social studies sections of a new Exit-Level TAAS. If you don't pass a section of this test the first time, you must retake it until you receive a passing score.

# Chapter 1

# TEST-TAKING STRATEGIES

## HOW TEST-TAKING STRATEGIES ARE LIKE A SWISS ARMY KNIFE

This chapter will provide you with the test-taking strategies you'll need in order to succeed on the TAAS. You might even be using some of these techniques already, but there's a big difference between using test-taking strategies *some* of the time and using them *all* of the time, for every subject test.

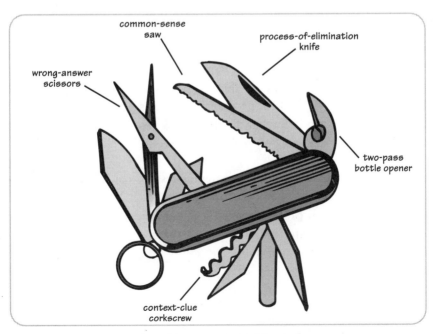

*A multi-purpose test-taking tool*

In this respect test-taking strategies are like that Swiss Army knife you got for Christmas: If you look at it just once and then put it in a drawer, it will never help you. If you occasionally carry it around with you, you might find some use for it, but it's more likely you'll forget it's there and not use it when a situation arises. However, if you take the knife and examine how all the different parts can be used, then you'll find you have the perfect tool for many different occasions.

This same premise holds true for the following test-taking strategies. If you take the time and practice using all of these techniques, you'll help yourself out on each TAAS subject test, and on other standardized tests you'll take in the future.

## Strategy 1

Know the format of each TAAS subject test before test day.

Before test day arrives, it's important to know how each test is structured—such as how many multiple-choice questions there are, what topics are covered, and how many correct answers you'll need to pass. By learning these things in advance, you'll help eliminate some of the anxiety you might be feeling about the test. Not only that, you'll even feel empowered by this knowledge, since the TAAS won't surprise and upset you. However, by not learning what you can beforehand, the Grade 8 TAAS remains a mysterious exam for which you'll probably feel a little nervous.

In terms of a Swiss Army knife, knowing the test format is like using the little magnifying glass that pops out of the far end. It lets you examine the TAAS up close so you can understand it better. The format of each subject test will be discussed later in the book, but for now you should familiarize yourself with the following facts.

**KAPLAN**

### The Big Four Format Facts

1. **TAAS tests are untimed.**

   Although you will have all day to take a single test, this is not recommended. Mental fatigue will inevitably set in, as will sheer boredom. So while the tests are untimed, try to spend only about 1 or 2 hours on each.

2. **The questions are all multiple-choice with four possible answer choices, with two exceptions.**

   These exceptions are:

   - Writing TAAS: Part 2, which is an essay, and
   - The final 60% of the questions on the Math TAAS. Starting around question 25, there will be *five* possible answer choices available. This will be explained more fully in chapter 3.

3. **About 15% of the questions on the TAAS will not count toward your score.**

   Your test will include what are called *field-test questions*. The Texas Education Agency (TEA) includes these for the purpose of trying out questions for future TAAS tests. On the one hand, this is helpful because it ensures test consistency from year to year. On the other hand, it also means that you'll spend about 15 percent of your time solving problems that won't help your score one jot. And since there's no way to identify them, it's impossible to skip them!

4. **The question breakdown on each subject test is consistent from year to year.**

   The following chart details the number of questions that count toward your score, and the number of correct answers you'll need to pass each test.

| Subject | Number of Multiple-Choice Questions* | Minimum Number Needed to Pass |
|---|---|---|
| Reading | 48 | 37 |
| Math | 60 | 45 |
| Science | 40 | 30 |
| Social Studies | 40 | 32 |
| Writing | 40 (and 1 essay) | 26/2** |

\* These numbers do not include additional field-test questions. They reflect only the questions that count toward your score.

\*\* The multiple-choice and essays scores are interdependent. How well you do on the essay will determine how many multiple-choice questions you'll need to get right. The higher your essay score, the fewer the multiple-choice questions you'll need to answer correctly. But you'll need to score at least a 2 on the essay, on a scale of 1–4 (highest).

## Strategy 2

Don't spend too much time on any one question at the expense of the rest of the test.

You won't be able to distinguish the field-test questions from the common items, so don't bother trying. Still, just knowing that 15 percent of the questions will have no affect on your score can help you in an important way: *Don't spend too much time on any one question.* On many tests you take in school, you try to get the highest grade possible by answering every question—no matter how long it takes. This isn't a good idea on the TAAS! Here, there are only two real grades: Pass or Fail. Spending too much time on a single question means you've wasted precious minutes and increased your mental fatigue greatly for a question that's worth about $\frac{1}{60}$ of your score. The fact of the matter is, there's a chance that the question is even a field-test question, which means you'd spend unnecessary time on a question that won't even count toward your score.

*An older Texas student berates himself for taking too long on a question.*

## Strategy 3

Maintain a consistent pace throughout the test. Don't rush through—or spend too long on—any one question.

The best way to avoid spending too long on any one question is to maintain a consistent pace throughout the test, never spending too much or too little time on any question. Proper pacing is something that all good test takers do naturally, but that can be learned quite easily by everyone else. Here are the ingredients you'll need to succeed at pacing.

## Mom's Old-Fashioned Pacing Recipe

Ingredients:

1. Two eyes (one eye will do as well.)

2. A watch.
   A digital watch or stopwatch is preferable, since it provides a more accurate display. Sundials and grand-father clocks are not a good choice.

Directions:

Use ingredient 1 to look at ingredient 2. Repeat often so that you have an accurate idea of how many questions are left, and how much remaining time you have to work on them.

Granted, pacing sounds simple, but in the heat of the moment this is one test-taking strategy that people often abandon first—usually with negative consequences. It's important to practice pacing *before* you take the test. By doing so, you'll get a sense of how much time you'll need to answer certain question types—and you'll be able to practice time management techniques for other areas of your life as well. Even though the tests are untimed, you don't want to go into overload by dragging them out, and keeping a steady pace will help you avoid mental fatigue.

Specific pacing tips for each TAAS subject test will be discussed in the appropriate chapters, but for now keep this game plan in mind.

## Strategy 4

Spend about 2 or 3 minutes on each multiple-choice question.

You want to spend enough time on a multiple-choice question so that you've carefully considered the answer choices and you haven't breezed through, but not so much time that you're laboring over the problem. Remember, your state-of-mind and energy level during the test are just as important as how much content you know.

Knowing about the test and setting a proper pace for yourself will help you take control of the TAAS. Think of it as a game plan, which is much better than just showing up and scribbling frantically once the exam begins.

Now that you know how much time you're going to spend on each question, the next step is deciding what order to do the questions in.

## Strategy 5

Do all the easy questions before you tackle the harder questions.

Why spend time on a hard question when there are easier questions—and easier points—waiting for you after it? Use a *two-pass system* on every TAAS session:

1. On the first pass, answer all the easy questions.

   If you come to a multiple-choice problem that stumps you, after a couple of minutes just move on. You can always come back to it, and there's no reason to get bogged down when there are easier points awaiting you.

2. On the second pass, start again at the beginning and go through the challenging, more time-consuming questions.

On the first pass, you want to concentrate on answering the questions you know, or can easily figure out, while on the second pass, you want to work the more difficult problems. If you're working at a consistent pace, you should spend more time on the second pass since it is the more involved part.

First I cut down the easy stuff, then I go back and chop the harder stuff.

© 2000 PhotoSpin Inc.

*A farmer considers how to use the two-pass system on his crops.*

If you're wondering how to tell a hard TAAS question from an easy question, the answer is simple: A hard question is one which you think is hard, and an easy question is one you think is easy. If you find yourself staring at a geometry question, and you have no idea how to solve it, then that's a hard question. Don't get too upset about it; just move on and answer the questions that follow. You can come back to that problem on the second pass, and give it more scrutiny.

Let's say that on the second pass, you reread the problem, but it still doesn't make sense to you. Should you skip it and move on? The answer is "Absolutely not!"

## Strategy 6

Answer every question, even if you have to guess. You won't lose points for any wrong answers, so any question you leave blank is a missed opportunity to boost your score.

Some tests, like the SAT, deduct any wrong answers from your total score. But the TAAS does no such thing—even if you had an impossibly hard question.

1.  What is the proper motion of Barnard's star*?
    A. 14 millibreems

    B. 10.25 arc seconds a year

    C. 6.12 star miles

    D. The Treaty of Ghent

Question 1 is incredibly difficult, but even if you have to guess, there's still a one in four chance you'll get it right. If you do get it right, it won't matter that it was a guess; all that matters is that the proper oval has been filled in.

Of course, instead of randomly guessing on a very tough problem, there's a strategy to help you improve your odds when guessing.

* The answer is B. This question is much tougher than those on the Science TAAS.

## Strategy 7

Use the Process of Elimination to help you find the answer.

If test-taking strategies are like a Swiss Army knife, then the Process of Elimination (POE) is the biggest, strongest knife in the set. POE is something most students know about, but rarely use, preferring instead to use their *recollection* and *knowledge* to answer questions. However, since a multiple-choice answer *is already in front of you*, this isn't always a necessary step. After all, what matters is that you select the correct answer. Knowing an answer to a question outright is great, but if that fails, POE is the most effective tool you can use to get the correct answer anyway. Look at the following two questions.

2. Who was the thirteenth president of the United States?
   Place your answer here. _____

3. Who was the thirteenth president of the United States?
   A. Abraham Lincoln

   B. Leo Tolstoy

   C. Millard Fillmore

   D. Chuckles the Clown

On question 2, if you don't know the answer, you have almost no chance of getting it right. However, on question 3, you can use POE and eliminate any answer choices you believe are incorrect. D is out, and if there was ever a president named Tolstoy, you would have remembered it, so B is out as well. That leaves A or C—at this point, it's a fifty-fifty shot, so take a guess and move on. Not every answer you guess on will be right, but provided you use POE regularly and effectively, you'll get enough right to boost your score.

Common sense is an important part of POE. In question 3, common sense tells you that America would never elect a clown to be a president (although some U.S. historians would tell you that Warren G. Harding comes pretty close).

In question 4 below, common sense can help you eliminate some answer choices.

4. Feinberg Fabrics uses the following price list for its cotton sheets.

| Area | Price |
|------|-------|
| 3 cm$^2$ | $6.00 |
| 6 cm$^2$ | $9.30 |
| 9 cm$^2$ | $12.90 |
| 12 cm$^2$ | $16.80 |

Based on this information, what would an 18 cm$^2$ sheet likely cost?

A. $12.00

B. $16.60

C. $18.60

D. $25.50

Before you start working out the math, use common sense and POE first. Looking at the prices, if a 12 cm$^2$ cotton sheet costs $16.80, will a larger sheet (18 cm$^2$) cost *more* or *less* than that? Common sense tells us it will cost *more*. Therefore, the answer will have to be *more than* $16.80, which is the price of the 12 cm$^2$ sheet. Using POE, then, you can get rid of A and B, since they're both less than $16.80. At his point, you can guess between C and D. Looking at the price list, you might note how the price appears to jump by about 3 or 4 dollars at each interval. Choice C is only about two dollars greater than $16.80, so D would be a safer bet. And it's the right answer!

POE is effective on all the TAAS subject tests. Look back to question 1, the Barnard's star question. If you had to eliminate one answer choice, which one would it be? Perhaps you'll see that D, The Treaty of Ghent, doesn't seem to have much to do with stars or motion, so it can be ruled out. You've just improved your guessing odds to one-in-three.

Besides common sense, there are other strategies for eliminating wrong answer choices.

Many students rush through standardized tests in an attempt to answer all the questions. This means they don't spend enough time considering each problem—if they see an answer choice that *looks* right, they quickly pick it and rush on. This is why you should take the full 1 or 2 minutes on each multiple-choice question, even if you see an answer that seems right in 15 seconds. Let's look at question 3 again.

3. Who was the thirteenth president of the United States?
   A. Abraham Lincoln

   B. Leo Tolstoy

   C. Millard Fillmore

   D. Chuckles the Clown

> If an answer choice looks too good to be true, it often is.

Of these four names, there is one president that almost everybody recognizes: Abraham Lincoln. If you were in a hurry, this question would take 15 seconds, since you would read the question and immediately pick the first (and perhaps only) name you recognized.

If you understand how the TAAS works, and how to attack standardized tests properly, you won't make that mistake. Using POE, you could eliminate B and D, as you did earlier. That leaves A and C, and frankly, A is just too good to be true. That leaves C, so Millard Fillmore must have been the thirteenth president of the United States.

> Look back at question 1. Do you see an answer choice that looks too good to be true? Since the word *star* appears in both the question and in choice C, you might be tempted to select C. It is not, however, the right answer.

Since multiple-choice questions make up almost the entire Grade 8 TAAS, using POE effectively can be a great boon to your score. Throughout this book, be sure your test your POE skills on every multiple-choice question you work on. There are also POE techniques specific to the subject tests, and they'll be discussed in the appropriate chapters.

## Strategy 8

Be of sound (and well-rested) mind and body on test day.

All of the studying and practice you do for the TAAS could be lost if you show up on test day cranky, tired, and hungry. Getting a good night's sleep and a complete, healthy breakfast are essential if you want to do well on the exams. It's hard to concentrate on a test when your stomach is grumbling so loud it sounds like Mozart's *Requiem Mass* is being performed in your duodenum. Make sure you eat a good breakfast, but don't eat so heavily that you find yourself dying for a nap. A bowl of cereal, toast, and fruit is a good way to start the day, and if your school will allow it, bring along a neat snack of some sort.

> A positive attitude on test day is worth more than any single fact you might study the night before the test.

In addition to a good meal, a good night's rest is vital to having a clear head on test day. This means no cramming! Staying up late into the night studying for the test is not a good idea, since this type of behavior often just adds to your anxiety level.

Do your studying ahead of time, so that your confidence is at its highest right before the test. If you want to do some review on the day before, focus on the format of the subject test you'll be taking, and on general test-taking strategies. This will help you more than cramming specific subject matter.

On the night before the test, do something relaxing that will take your mind off the upcoming exam. Extreme sports is probably not the best idea, nor is exhausting yourself physically. Play a board game with family or friends, or watch a video. Or if you like, take a short walk or a quick hike in a nearby park. But remember, if you do go on a hike, be sure to bring along your Swiss Army knife and use it in as many ways as possible.

## Strategy Review

Strategy 1:  Know the format of each TAAS subject test before test day.

Strategy 2:  Don't spend too much time on any one question at the expense of the rest of the test.

Strategy 3:  Maintain a consistent pace throughout the test. Don't rush through—or spend too long on—any one question.

Strategy 4:  Spend about 2 or 3 minutes on each multiple-choice question.

Strategy 5:  Do all the easy questions before you tackle the harder questions.

Strategy 6:  Answer every question, even if you have to guess. You won't lose points for any wrong answers, so any question you leave blank is a missed opportunity to boost your score.

Strategy 7:  Use the Process of Elimination (POE) to help you find the answer.

Strategy 8:  Be of sound (and well-rested) mind and body on test day.

**KAPLAN**

# Chapter 2

# READING

## HOW ANSWERING TAAS READING QUESTIONS IS LIKE COMING UP WITH SEVEN SYNONYMS FOR *SQUEAL*

From memory, can you come up with seven words that mean the same thing as *squeal*? *Cry* is a good choice, and so are *scream* and *yell*. *Shriek* makes four synonyms, and after that . . . well, there's always *grumpy*, *sneezy*, and *bashful*. Wait, those last three are the Seven Dwarves, not seven synonyms.

Coming up with seven definitions for *squeal* by memory is not an easy task. But what if you were asked the same question, yet this time you could use a thesaurus to help you? Since a thesaurus is a reference book devoted to synonyms, the task becomes much easier: Just thumb through the thesaurus until you reach *squeal*, and look at all the synonyms. You'll come up with *cry, scream, yell, shriek, wail, yelp,* and *whine*, not to mention *shrill, screech, peep, bawl,* and *squeak.*

It's obviously easier to refer to the thesaurus than to use your memory. The same holds true for the Reading TAAS. It's common for students to read a passage and attempt the questions from memory, but this isn't a good idea. It's like struggling to think of seven synonyms for *squeal* when you have a thesaurus sitting in front of you. On this section of the TAAS, you need to treat all the reading passages like the thesaurus, and continually refer to them.

### Strategy

The answer to every reading question lies somewhere in the passage, and that's where you should always look.

You might not feel like looking back at the passage for each and every question, as it's time-consuming and seems to be wasted effort. You might think, "Why should I look back? The answer is right in front of me!" That might be true, but it's also true that three wrong answers in front of you. The questions are actually designed to trip you up if you don't refer to the text.

*Trying to answer TAAS Reading questions without referring to the passage can lead you into a big hole.*

## Reading TAAS Facts

During the Reading TAAS, you'll read a passage and then answer questions about it. There will be approximately 6 or 7 passages. You'll likely see some of the following passage formats:

- nonfiction excerpt
- fiction excerpt
- excerpt from a play
- short biography
- two letters
- an advertisement
- a poster
- classified ads excerpt

Of course, there's no guarantee that the reading passages on your test won't be six consecutive advertisements, but since there's a great deal of consistency from year to year, you'll probably see two fiction excerpts, two non-fiction excerpts (quite likely a biography), and then two or three unusual passages (such as a poster or classified ad.) While these odd passages may look strange, treat them in the same way you would approach any other passage. There's no reason that the unusual format should rattle you.

As far as how many questions you'll see, there are approximately 7–9 questions per passage. You have two options for going through them:

> You can answer the questions in whatever order you want, so be sure to take advantage of this fact.

1. Go through all the passages that have the most questions first, and then go back from the start and tackle those with fewer questions; or

2. If you prefer to read fiction over non-fiction (or vice versa), answer all the fiction passages first, and then hit the non-fiction and other passages. Either approach works.

Although the number of questions per passage remains fairly consistent from year to year, the length of the passages varies. Some poems will have no more than 400 words, while other passages can clock in at 800 words. The average passage length is about 600 words, as you might expect. Because there's such a great range among the reading passages, there's no hard-and-fast pacing rule that you can establish as you read. You can't say, "I'll spend 5 minutes reading the passage every time" since that would leave you rushing through the 800-word passage and wasting time on the 400-word text. Even so, there's something you should keep in mind:

---

### Strategy

Read to understand, not to memorize, each passage. The point of the session is to answer the questions, not to read the passages. Even if it's the most fascinating topic, don't spend unnecessary time poring over the text.

---

As you read through a text, read with an eye toward overall comprehension, not toward memorization. It's more important to understand the main idea and overall development of a passage than it is to place details into your long-term memory. Get the main idea, picking up on things like tone and the author's point of view. Then, focus in on where supporting storylines/details/facts are located—for instance, paragraph 2 deals with snakes, while paragraph 3 is about ladders. Then, head to the questions. That way, if a question is a main idea question, you'll be in good shape answering it, and if the next question asks about ladders, you'll know where to look— in paragraph 3, since it deals with ladders.

By having a general idea of where the details are located in a passage, you'll be able to head right to the text that will enable you to answer a question. To help you do this, jot down notes about the passage as you read it the first time. The notes don't need to be intricate details relating exactly what occurs in each paragraph, but they should act as markers to remind you of what's in each section. These markers will help you to answer questions more quickly, and answering questions is what the TAAS is all about.

## The Big Five

If the TAAS were an un-standardized test, a book like this would be impossible to write. One year the TAAS might be all essays, the next year it might consist of just fill-in-the-blank questions, and the year after that the TAAS could be nothing more than a teacher standing in front of you asking, "Guess what number I'm thinking of now."

Fortunately, the TAAS is a standardized test, and that means that the major question types remain consistent from year to year. There are six multiple-choice question types on the reading test, but we'll call them the Big Five because numbers 4 and 5 require a similar approach. The question types are listed below.

| TAAS Objective | Number of Questions on Reading TAAS* |
|---|---|
| 1. Word Meanings | 4 |
| 2. Supporting Ideas | 4 |
| 3. Summarization | 8 |
| 4. Relationships and Outcomes | 8 |
| 5. Inferences and Generalizations | 16 |
| 6. Point of View, Propaganda, Fact, and Nonfact | 8 |
| **Total number of questions** | 48 |
| **Minimum needed for passing score** | 32 correct answers |

* These numbers do not include the 8 field-test questions, which do not count toward your score.

Knowing in advance the exact question breakdown is a great benefit, so take some time to study the chart above. Obviously, you wouldn't want to spend all your time learning about Word Meaning Questions at the expense of Inference Questions, since Inference Questions outnumber Word Meaning Questions four to one.

Before we look more closely at the six question types, let's see a sample reading passage. Remember that your goal is to understand, not to memorize.

*The following excerpt has been adapted from Act I, Scene 2 from* The Duchess of Malfi *by John Webster, published in 1623.*

| | |
|---|---|
| *Delio*: | Then the law to the duke |
| | Is like a foul black cobweb to a spider, |
| | He makes it his dwelling and a prison |
| | To entangle those shall feed him. |

| | | |
|---|---|---|
| *Antonio*: | Most true: | [5] |
| | He never pays debts unless they be shrewd turns, | |
| | And those he will confess that he doth owe. | |
| | Last, for his brother there, the cardinal, | |
| | They that do flatter him most say oracles | |
| | Hang at his lips; and truly I believe them, | [10] |
| | For the darkness speaks in them. | |
| | But for their sister, the right noble duchess, | |
| | You never fix'd your eye on three fair medals, | |
| | Cast in one figure, of so different temper. | |
| | For her discourse, it is so full of rapture, | [15] |
| | You only will begin then to be sorry | |
| | When she does end her speech, and wish, in wonder, | |
| | She held it less vain-glory, to talk much, | |
| | Than your penance to hear her: while she speaks, | |
| | She throws upon a man so sweet a look, | [20] |
| | That it were able to raise one to a dance | |
| | That lay in a dead palsy. | |
| | . . . | |

| | |
|---|---|
| *Delio*: | Fie, Antonio, |
| | You play yourself out with her commendation. |

| | | |
|---|---|---|
| *Antonio*: | I'll case the picture up, only thus much, | [25] |
| | All her particular worth grows to this sum; | |
| | She stains the time past: lights the time to come. | |

## Using POE

The reading passages on the TAAS have been chosen or written by educators. Since this is the case, you'll never read an essay that talks about how to win at gambling or a poem that describes how robbing banks is fun. Instead, you'll read passages that are informa-

> Don't be afraid to use the strategies you've learned for one type of question on other, unfamiliar types of questions.

tive, educational, and often strive to make a positive point. So when trying to eliminate wrong answer choices, you can safely assume that anything too extreme or negative can be ruled out. This won't be the case *every* time, but more often than not it will.

### Strategy

On the Reading TAAS, cross out answer choices that are too extreme or negative. Look for choices that are bland, somewhat positive, and easier to prove. You won't be able to do this in every case, but it's a safe bet if you're stuck.

Look at the following question:

1. What concept about Julius and Garcon is most thoroughly developed in the passage?
   A. Both men came from wealthy families.

   B. The two men had nothing at all in common.

   C. The two men represented different cultures.

   D. Julius and Garcon hated each other.

You know absolutely nothing about the passage that accompanied this question, but try crossing out answer choices that are too extreme or negative. Which ones would you pick? Choice B is rather extreme—if the two men had just one thing in common, it would be wrong, so B should be crossed out. D is pretty harsh, and while there's a slim chance it could be true, your best bet on the TAAS is to cross it out. That leaves A and C, which gives you a fifty-fifty shot on a question for which you never even saw the passage. Let's try another one.

2. What is the best inference that can be made from the Governor's statement?

A. There was some confusion after the hurricane.

B. People were scared to go the disaster shelters.

C. Most people were robbing stores downtown.

D. Absolute panic had broken out throughout the city.

Eliminating extreme or negative answers on this question should lead to the right answer. C is not a good choice because it uses the word *most*—this implies a majority of people. In order for C to be correct, there would have to be a place in the passage that said that 51 percent or more of the people were robbing, and this seems both extreme and too negative for the TAAS. D has the same problem, with the word *absolute*. What if some people were only half-panicked? There goes your *absolute*. Choice D is also not very positive.

That leaves A and B. Choice A is good because it has the bland word "some" in it. *Some* can mean a little, or it could mean a lot, but it's fairly vague and therefore easy to prove. If just one person is confused, that means there's "some confusion." As for B, a dose of common sense—always useful when using POE throughout the TAAS—will cast this answer choice into a bad light. Why would people be afraid to seek a disaster shelter after a hurricane? It makes little sense. Of course, there's a slight chance that B is correct, but A is by far your best choice here. And guess what? It's the correct answer.

As you look over the following multiple-choice questions about the Big Five Question Types, keep in mind the following: "Are there any answer choices that I could eliminate using POE?" If you practice POE to the point where it becomes second nature, it will benefit you on the test. If you read about it now but never use it again, it won't be as useful, and your score will likely suffer.

## The Big Five Multiple-Choice Question Types

### 1. Word Meaning Questions (4 questions per test)

Designed to test your vocabulary, there may be several questions on the Reading TAAS that ask, "What does _____ mean?" To answer these questions correctly, you'll need to either:

> A. know the definition of the word already; or
> B. figure out the meaning of the word from the words and phrases around it.

Option A is just nifty, but option B is a highly useful test-taking skill, so we'll focus on that. Option B, also called *learning in context*, is something everyone can do. To illustrate this, look at question 3.

> 3. Joan said, "Please get the *sargfrommanhemmar* from the fridge and serve some to our guests, who are no doubt very hungry." What does *sargfrommanhemmar* mean?
>
>    A. It is a type of food.
>
>    B. It is a highly venomous sea snake.
>
>    C. It is a type of drink.
>
>    D. It is a statue made out of clay.

Based on Joan's sentence, which answer would you choose? If you choose A, you'd be right. (If you choose B, you probably won't have many guests living much longer.) Using the words around *sargfrommanhemmar*, you were able to deduce that it is a type of food, which is why it was in the fridge. Choice C is a close second guess, but why would you give a drink to people who are hungry? If you replace the word *hungry* with *thirsty* in the original sentence, choice C becomes a better answer.

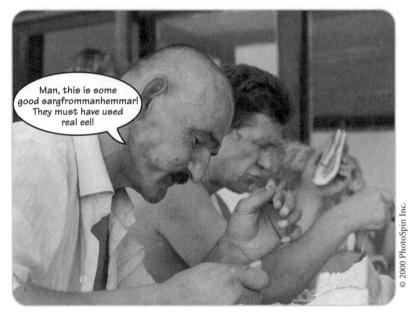

*After a day of testing, the locals relax and enjoy a bowl of sargfrommanhemmar at Newt's Backway Eatery.*

The words you'll be asked to define in Word Meaning Questions will always be underlined within the passage. So when you see an underlined word, you'll know that there's an upcoming question about it. You might want to answer a question like this immediately after you read the underlined word in the passage, so that the context of the word is fresh in your mind. Or, perhaps you feel that breaking off to answer a question is too much of an interruption, so you'd prefer reading the entire passage before you attack the questions. Either approach is fine; just be careful to stick to one or the other, though, so you don't lose track of the task at hand.

This is what it means to keep a steady pace throughout the test—you don't want to be using one approach for one passage, and another approach for another passage. Having to flip back and forth to reorganize and refocus will only break your concentration. Think about what test-taking approaches you're comfortable with beforehand and plan to use them consistently on the test.

## Strategy

When you're trying to define a new word, look at what the words and phrases *around* it mean to see how it fits into the sentence.

For question 4, check back to the *Duchess of Malfi* passage on page 26.

4. In line 22, what does the word *palsy* mean?
   A. eager to dance

   B. prepared to fight

   C. ready to flee

   D. unable to move

When you refer to the text, don't just read the line that has *palsy* in it; always start two or three lines before and read through to the sentence that follows. You want to make sure that you grasp the full context of the word, and you can only do that by reading several sentences around it. By now, you probably recognize from the passage that the 'Duchess is a really beautiful, wonderful woman,' or something along those lines. With this as your framework, looking over lines 20–23 you'll see that since she is so beautiful and kind, she could make someone dance who had been . . . *unable to move*, choice D.

Another approach here would be to use Elimination. Some wrong answer choices are meant to mislead you, so be careful not to rush through seemingly easy questions. For example, in question 4, choice A has the word *dance* in it; since the line that comes immediately before line 23 also has the word *dance* in it, you might incorrectly be tempted to choose it. Cross it out instead. Then, using common sense, you might notice that line 23 actually says *dead palsy*, and this makes B and C unlikely answer choices because how could somebody be *dead* and *prepared to fight* or *flee* at the same time? You can be *dead* and *unable to move*, however.

### 2. Supporting Idea Questions (4 questions per test)

Supporting Idea Questions focus on small facts that you would be unlikely to remember if you read the passage just once. You'll always find the answers to these question *directly in the passage*, so the key is to refer to it as much as is needed. Here's a good example.

> A man in a blue business suit walks into a bank wearing a large green duck on his head. The bank teller looks at him and asks, "Is it hard to keep that thing balanced like that?"
>
> "Not really," replied the duck. "I've got sticky, webbed feet."

Supporting Idea Questions related to the story above might be, "What color was the man's suit?" or "What size was the duck?"

---

**Strategy**

To answer Supporting Idea Questions, you'll need to go back and look at the passage.

---

Other than that, there's nothing too difficult about these problems. The main pitfall for this question type is when you *sort of* remember an answer, and one of the answer choices *looks* right, so you pick it. But it's wrong! There's no point in trying to answer these questions from memory—it will only hurt your score.

5. In the story, the Duke and the Duchess are
   A. married.

   B. similar in appearance.

   C. related by birth.

   D. both friends of the Cardinal.

The key is to find the correct part of the passage that contains the information you need. This is why, when reading the passage for the first time, you want to get a general idea of what events occur when. If you do that well, you'll be able to head straight to the line that says "But for their sister," and you'll see that choice C is correct.

### 3. Summarization Questions (8 questions per test)

As you might expect, reading a passage through to glean its main idea is very helpful on Summarization Questions. Sometimes these questions just ask for the main idea, but it's quite possible you'll be asked how specific parts of the passage fit into the entire reading.

6. Which of the following statements best describes the passage?

   A. The Duchess is a good person, but her brothers are not.

   B. The Duke and Cardinal are completely evil.

   C. Most people love the Duchess more than the Duke.

   D. The Duke rarely pays his debts.

7. Delio gives a description of the Duke, while Antonio gives a description of

   A. the Duchess only.

   B. the Duchess and the Cardinal.

   C. the Duke, Duchess, and the Cardinal.

   D. the Duke only.

Question 6 is a fairly straightforward Main Idea Question, while question 7 asks for the main idea of Antonio's monologue. In other words, while question 6 refers to the entire reading, question 7 probes whether you have understood the idea and general outline of a specific part of the reading.

### Strategy

On Summarization Questions, look for answer choices that state the big picture and eliminate answer choices that are too small in scope.

Summarization Questions address the big picture of a passage, so you can safely rule out answer choices that are very detailed or specific. Compare answer choices A and D in question 6. Both statements are true, according to the text, but D is just one small fact. Choice A is a broader statement that covers the entire reading. Watch out for misleading answer choices, which are frequently included to trap you. Misleading (and wrong) answer choices might be accurate facts from the passage; the catch is that they're not broad enough to be the main point. Choice B is too extreme, since "completely evil" is impossible to prove—what if the Cardinal liked to help lost puppies, and the Duke was devoted to preserving the rainforest? That would mean they're not *completely* evil, even though they appear to be pretty bad.

Choice C in question 6 represents another type of wrong answer choice (a trap!) commonly seen on Summarization Questions: the *probably true* statement. From what you can infer from the text, chances are that you think the duchess is a likeable person, but where is that stated in the passage? The answer: Nowhere. This is why referring to the passage is always a good idea. If you suspected choice C was right, you'd have to be able to back it up—but nowhere do the characters mention that the citizens of Malfi love the Duchess more than the Duke. So while there's a good chance that that's true, you can't safely conclude that.

Question 7 might be very easy if you had jotted down notes to yourself as you read the passage. You might have written "duke = bad," "cardinal = evil," and "duchess = kind, pretty" in the margins of the text. If you did, then you're in good shape but if not, it's just a matter of referring to the passage to see who Antonio talks about. This would be a wise move, because if you don't, you might only remember what Delio said about the Duke and then pick B. In fact, Delio talks more about the Duke than Antonio, but Antonio mentions the Duke, the Cardinal and the Duchess. The question asks *who* the characters have described, not *how much* is described. The correct answer is C.

## 4. Inference Questions

### Relationships and Outcomes (8 questions per test)
### Inferences and Generalizations (16 questions per test)

A broad question category, Inference Questions are simply questions whose answers are not stated directly in the passage. Instead, you have to infer the answer from what you have read. For instance, although the *Duchess of Malfi* passage never specifically states the Cardinal is evil, you can infer this from the phrase "the darkness speaks in them."

To some degree, answering an Inference Question is like answering a Vocabulary Question. In order to define a new vocabulary word, you must find clues in the surrounding words. Similarly, for Inference Questions, you need to locate clues in the passage that will help you draw a conclusion about something that has been written and then answer the question.

While the TEA separates *Relationships & Outcome* and *Inference & Generalizations* questions into two categories, the strategies for approaching them are identical. For the purposes of instruction, this book combines the two question types into a single Inference category.

8. According to Antonio, how did most people react when the Duchess stopped talking?
   A. They were disappointed.
   B. They were angry.
   C. They wanted to dance.
   D. They were struck by love.

Using POE, you can eliminate some choices before you even look at the passage. Since you know that the Duchess was a good person from your first read-through, B is an unlikely choice. Choice C takes the word *dance* directly from the passage, but from a reference Antonio makes about the duchess's *looks*, not her *speech*. About her speech, Antonio states "You only will begin, then, to be sorry/When she doth end her speech." This is the clue that should lead you to choice A, *disappointed*, which comes closest to that meaning.

Again, since the answer is not actually spelled out in the passage, you'll have to read between the lines and select the answer choice that comes closest.

> ## Strategy
>
> On Inference Questions, find the clues in the passage that will help you determine the answer. Remember, since it won't be spelled out in the text, you'll have to infer the answer.

Another type of Inference Question is the Emotions Question, which asks you to figure out the emotional state of the author or a character in the passage. Once again, as with the other Inference Questions, you have to determine the person's emotional state from clues in the text. However, since the TAAS is written by educators, a good fallback position on these questions is to look for a happy, positive answer, and then pick it.

9.  What emotion does Antonio appear to feel about the Duchess?

    A. friendship

    B. hatred

    C. mistrust

    D. admiration

10. Which word best describes the character of the Duke?

    A. nurturing

    B. petty

    C. devious

    D. pious

Question 9 shows how you can sometimes get an answer without even looking at a passage, while question 10 shows that it always helps to check your answers by looking back at the reading. For question 9, choices B and C, *hatred* and *mistrust*, are both negative, so they're likely to be incorrect. That leaves A and D, and while it's a bit of a toss-up in terms of positivity, D is the correct answer.

As useful as the "choose the most broad and positive answer choice" strategy is, you can't apply it in every case. On question 10, if you hadn't read the passage you might want to guess between A and D, both positive attributes. But since the duke is a bad man, having been compared to a "spider in foul, black cobweb," that won't work here. The answer is B or C, and from the spider reference you'll hopefully infer that *devious* is a better choice than merely *petty*.

> On questions that ask you to determine the emotional state of the author or a character in the text, answers tend not to be *extreme* or *negative*. Look for an answer choice that is broad and uplifting/educational.

### 5. Point of View, Propaganda, Fact and Nonfact Questions (8 questions per test)

There are eight questions that fall under the cumbersome title of Point of View, Propaganda, Fact and Nonfact, but 2–4 of them will simply ask, "Which is a FACT in the passage?" POE works especially well for those, because they usually include 1 or 2 answer choices that are clearly wrong and can be crossed out immediately. They're wrong answer choices because they express *opinions*, not facts. They contain words like *excited, easier, faster, enjoys, superior, unlucky, thinks,* and *courageous*—all subjective opinions. Even though most people believe that "eating a cracker is *easier* than scaling Mt. Everest in a bathrobe," that doesn't make it a fact, because there's no way to conclusively prove it.

Here's another example. Look at the related statements below, and decide which are facts and which are opinions.

1. Michael Jordan was the greatest basketball player ever.
2. Michael Jordan was a great basketball player.
3. Michael Jordan won multiple NBA scoring titles.
4. Michael Jordan won a whole bunch of NBA scoring titles.
5. Michael Jordan has appeared in a movie.
6. Michael Jordan is the greatest actor ever.

Statement 1 is extreme, and 2 is a more modified version of 1. However, both 1 and 2 are opinions, because you can't *prove* that a person is great. 3 is a fact that can be proven, but contrast this with 4, which you can't prove because the phrase "a whole bunch" is open to interpretation. Statement 5 is a fact, but as for 6 . . . well, let's just say that it is *definitely* not a fact.

So, let's try a question related to the *Duchess of Malfi* passage on page 26.

11. Which is a FACT in the passage?

A. The citizens of Malfi like the Duchess.

B. The Duchess of Malfi is an exceptional woman.

C. The Duchess and the Cardinal are related.

D. Antonio is in love with the Duchess.

Eliminating all answer choices that aren't facts should leave you with only one selection. While everything Antonio says about the Duchess is positive, that doesn't mean he's in love with her, so D can be crossed out. In order for D to be correct, you would have to have a way to prove *love*. For that matter, there's no way to tell how the citizens of Malfi feel about the Duchess, and so A is out as well. Again, how can you prove someone *likes* you? Along those same lines, how can you prove that someone is *exceptional*, since everyone has his own opinion about what constitutes that? Only choice C remains, the only fact that can be proven.

In addition to the 2–4 FACT questions, you'll also see a "Which is an OPIN-ION in this passage?" question on the Reading TAAS. Guess what? You answer these in the exact opposite way you answer the FACT questions. Look for the answer choice that is subjective and cannot be proved, and eliminate any choices that are facts that can be proved in the passage.

When you finish answering the questions, use any remaining time to check over your answers. First, make sure you haven't accidentally skipped any questions, and then, look carefully to make sure you bubbled in the correct oval on each question. Once you do that, you will have completed the Reading TAAS session. To celebrate this event, wait until the test is over, and then let out a squeal of delight. Or if you prefer, a *scream* of delight. Or a *yell, shriek, wail, yelp, whine, screech* . . .

# Chapter 3

# *MATH*

## HOW TAAS MATH IS LIKE
## WATCHING *BAYWATCH* IN NEPAL

Landlocked between India and Tibet and home to nine of the world's ten largest mountains, Nepal doesn't get a lot of sun 'n' surf. This could explain why many Nepalese find *Baywatch* such an interesting program, as it takes place in an area of the world that's very sunny and definitely non-Himalayan.

If you were to hang out in Kathmandu, Nepal's capital, you might catch an episode or two of the show. At first glance, the Nepali *Baywatch* would probably confuse you, since the characters would be speaking a language you're unfamiliar with. Yet once you got over your initial confusion, you would see that the show really isn't hard to follow—even in Nepalese. A lifeguard's job is to save drowning people, and this is true regardless of what language is being spoken. Watching *Baywatch* in Nepal is just like watching *Baywatch* in Texas; the characters still act the same way... if you call what they do "acting."

When you take the Math TAAS, you might come across a question so confusing that it looks like it's Nepalese in origin. If you let it rattle your nerves, chances are you'll lose confidence in your ability to solve it. But if you let your initial puzzlement pass, you should be able to figure out what the question is really asking. This is still a math test, and a fractions question is a fractions question, regardless of how it appears. Many students can't get past their anxiety in these situations, and their scores inevitably suffer. If you go into the test knowing that a few questions will appear Nepalese to you, you be able to refocus your thoughts with confidence and figure out what's being asked of you.

### Strategy

Some questions may look strange, but if you take the time to figure out what they're really asking, then doing well on them should be as easy as spending a day at the beach.

## Math TAAS Format

The Math test has 60 multiple-choice questions on it (plus 8 field test questions that don't count toward your score). Of the 60 questions, you'll need to get at least 40 questions right to pass the test.

The Texas Education Agency (TEA) has indicated that the minimum passing number of 40 out of 60 might change on future tests.

Now, 40 out of 60 translates to two-thirds, which means that if you can get *two* out of every *three* questions right, you pass the TAAS. While this doesn't mean you should be lazy and answer only two out of every three questions, it does mean that no single question is going to determine your grade. If you come to a hard question and can't figure it out, just move on and come back to it later.

The TAAS is untimed, but since most students are affected by the law of diminishing returns, you probably won't do as well in seventh hour of a test as you will during the first hour. On your first pass through the math questions, plan on spending 1 or 2 minutes on each. If you haven't figured out what to do with a question after 2 minutes, leave it for the second pass. When you do go back to it, give it another 3 minutes, but if you're still stuck after that, you're better off conserving your mental energy for other problems. Don't just skip it, though. Use Process of Elimination if possible, take a guess, and then move on. As they say, there are always more multiple-choice questions in the sea.

Speaking of questions, there are thirteen kinds of questions on the Math TAAS. The TAAS is designed by the TEA to see how well students have mastered the state's math curriculum, known as the *Texas Essential Knowledge and Skills* (TEKS). These thirteen TAAS Objectives are designed to match this curriculum.

| TAAS Objective | Number of Questions on Math TAAS* |
|---|:---:|
| 1. Number Concepts | 4 |
| 2. Algebraic/Math Relations & Functions | 4 |
| 3. Geometric Properties and Relationships | 4 |
| 4. Measurements Concepts | 4 |
| 5. Probabiltiy and Statistics | 4 |
| 6. Use of Additon to Solve Problems | 4 |
| 7. Use of Subtraction to Solve Problems | 4 |
| 8. Use of Multiplication to Solve Problems | 4 |
| 9. Use of Division to Solve Problems | 4 |
| 10. Problem Solving Using Estimation | 4 |
| 11. Problem Solving Using Solution Strategies | 8 |
| 12. Problem Solving Using Math Representation | 8 |
| 13. Evaluation of the Reasonableness of a Solution | 4 |

Now, thirteen different objectives might seem like a lot of material to learn, but the TEA has simplified things by testing only certain objectives on certain problems.

### The Math TAAS: A Tale of Three Tests

The TAAS Objectives listed above are grouped together in the following way:

| | |
|---|---|
| **Math Questions 1–20:** | **TAAS Objectives 1–5** |
| **Math Questions 21–44:** | **TAAS Objectives 10–13** |
| **Math Questions 45–60:** | **TAAS Objectives 6–94** |

The existence of field-test questions will throw these exact numbers off a little bit. For instance, TAAS Objectives 1–5 might go from questions 1–22 on the real test because of two added field-test questions. While this will throw off the question count a bit, the fact remains that there will be only 20 questions on Objectives 1–5 that DO count toward your score.

So you never have to worry about finding a question concerning TAAS Objective 1 on question 32, because it will never appear there. Instead, train your mind to think of the Math test as three different tests. Questions 1–20 will require certain kinds of math strategies and skills, and questions 21–44 and 45–60 will require other kinds. Overall, though, this breakdown works to your benefit, since all you need to do is be aware of these changes and prepare for them accordingly.

### Why You Don't Need to Memorize $S = 6s^2$

While many of you have probably spent long hours memorizing formulas such as the one above—which is the formula for the surface area of a cube—such diligence is not required for the TAAS. This is because your test booklet comes with a Math Reference Sheet that lists a load of formulas and conversions, free to use throughout the exam. These formulas are sure to come in handy, especially if you see a question like this:

1. If a rectangular prism has a volume of 896 cubic feet, and its length and width are each 8 feet, what is its height?

   A. 8 feet

   B. 12 feet

   C. 14 feet

   D. 16 feet

On a problem like this, the Reference Sheet can be very useful. First, write out the formula for the volume of a rectangular prism (also known as a *box)* which is V = *lwh*.

Many math problems require more than one step of work, and in order to ensure that you're on track every step of the way, you'll want to write everything out. This advice is extremely critical. Writing out all of your calculations will give you something to work from when you recheck your answers. After all, if you write nothing down, and merely calculate the numbers in your head, there's no way to catch any mistakes!

Calculators are *not* permitted, so you'll have to work out your calculations on paper. Don't just do the math in your head, or you'll be asking for trouble! Make sure you write everything out.

So, back to question 1, we have V = $l \times w \times h$. Now, substitute the numbers that you know:

$$896 = 8 \times 8 \times h$$
$$896 = 64 \times h$$
$$\frac{896}{64} = h$$
$$14 = h$$

The answer is C, 14 feet.

There are a few items on the Reference Sheet that you should know especially well. One is the **Pythagorean theorem**, which allows you find the length of the third side of a right triangle if you know the lengths of the other two sides. Another important item is the **Measurement Conversion** section, which provides various conversions for Metric and Standard units. This is important because there will most likely be 1–3 questions that ask you to convert different units.

*Unable to use the Reference Sheet, a woman stands at her doorway and hopes that 2(lw) + 2 (hw) + 2(lh) just happens to come walking down the street.*

## Process of Elimination on the Math TAAS

Imagine that on the Math test, the Process of Elimination was like a group of animals with two dominant species:

> **Species 1:** *Numeralis eliminatorius*
> This species allows you to eliminate answer choices that contain the same numbers used in the original question.

> **Species 2:** *Ballparkius nonsensicalus*
> This species allows you to eliminate answer choices that contain numbers which are obviously too high or low.

Both POE species can be found throughout the Math TAAS, and in shaded, woodland areas. These animals feed off of tubers, roots, and students who rush through the multiple-section of the test. Species 1, *Numeralis eliminatorius*, is especially fond of catching students, who, when confused by a question, pick the answer choice that has identical numbers to those in the problem. If captured and trained, both POE species make excellent test-taking techniques.

Here's an example of *Numeralis eliminatorius* in its native habitat.

2. Prakash is assembling a crib for his nephew. He tries a $\frac{3}{8}$ inch screw in one of the legs, but discovers that is it slightly too large. Which of the following screw sizes, in inches, is the next smaller one?

   A. $\frac{1}{8}$

   B. $\frac{5}{16}$

   C. $\frac{1}{2}$

   D. $\frac{5}{8}$

Let's say that you have no idea how to proceed, so with a quick glance over the answer choices, you see that A and D both contain 8 as the fraction's denominator. Since $\frac{3}{8}$ was in the problem itself, you would be tempted to pick A or D and be done with it. *You've just been eaten by Numeralis!* More often than not, an answer choice that has the same numbers as those in the question itself is *wrong*. These are trick answer choices, intended to catch you if you work too quickly through the test.

If you had no idea how to solve question 2, your best bet would be to cross out A and D and then take a guess.

## Strategy

Be wary of answer choices that contain the same numbers as those in the question. They're often traps designed to catch students who are in a hurry.

The other species of POE, *Ballparkius nonsensicalus*, can be found in question 3.

3. A hat contains 90 slips of paper that are either blue, red, or yellow. If half the slips are yellow, and the ratio of blue slips to red slips is 2 to 1, how many red slips are there?

A. 60

B. 45

C. 30

D. 15

Common sense can help uncover the incorrect *Ballparkius* answers. Before finding the specific number of red slips, ask yourself a few questions that will help you ballpark the correct figure. If half the slips are yellow, then how many yellow slips are there? The answer is half of 90, which is 45. That leaves 45 slips of red and blue paper combined. With this in mind, will the number of red slips be greater or less than 45?

You've probably figured out that there have to be *fewer than* 45 red slips, so choices A and B are both wrong. A is way off, since it's greater than 45. By estimating the correct answer, you used POE to eliminate *Ballparkius* answer choices.

Look at the two remaining answer choices, 30 and 15. Since the question states, "blue slips outnumber red slips by two to one," which one would you pick? If you choose D, 15, you would be correct, since 30 blue slips outnumber 15 red slips by two to one.

> **Strategy**
>
> POE is your most effective tool on math multiple-choice questions.

### The First Third: Questions 1-20

**TAAS Objective 1:**    Number Concepts (4 questions)

**TAAS Objective 2:**    Algebraic/Math Relationships and Functions (4 questions)

**TAAS Objective 3:**    Geometric Properties and Relationships (4 questions)

**TAAS Objective 4:**    Measurement Concepts (4 questions)

**TAAS Objective 5:**    Probability and Statistics (4 questions)

Of all the questions on the test, some of the easiest to recognize are those covering number concepts, measurement concepts, and geometry. For instance, Number Concept Questions test your understanding of a variety of basic math terms. Favorite topics include: percentages, number lines, mean and median, fractions, ratios, exponents, order of operations, greater than/less than, positive/negative numbers, and even number lines. If you just said "Huh?" to any of those topics, your first order of business is to learn that topic inside and out.

## Strategy

Problems involving simple math terms become simple to do if you are very familiar with the terms being used.

4. Following is a distribution of students at Cloverleaf High who are taking a foreign language.

| French | 44% |
|--------|-----|
| Spanish | 34% |
| German | 20% |
| Urdu | 2% |

If there 550 students taking a foreign language, how many of them would you expect to be taking French?

A. 308

B. 242

C. 110

D. 17

5. $(2 + 3 \times \sqrt{25})^2$ equals

A. 100

B. 289

C. 625

D. 900

Question 4 is a fairly straightforward percentage question. If you're familiar enough with percentages, you'll know to multiply the number of total students (550) by the percentage taking French (44%, or 0.44). This gives you 242, choice B. If you're not comfortable using percentages, and you'd rather use POE, you can eliminate some Ballparkius choices. For instance, half of 550 is 275. Since you're looking for 44%, you know the answer will be slightly less than 50%, or 275. So A is out, and D is way too small, leaving B and C. A good guess at this point should lead you to B.

Question 5 tests your knowledge of the proper order of operations. Just working from right to left will yield 625, but this is incorrect. In fact, the *25* indicates that this is a bit of *Numeralis eliminatorius*. Taking the square root of 25, multiplying it by 3, then adding 2, and finally squaring that number will get you choice B, 289.

The key to solving many Number Concept Questions is to know your basic math terms, and the key to solving many Measurement Concepts Questions is simply to use the Math Reference Sheet.

6. An aquarium pump is able to transmit one gallon of water every fifteen minutes. How many **quarts** of water is the pump able to move per hour?

   A. 1

   B. 4

   C. 15

   D. 16

Some Measurement Concepts Questions will ask you to convert one unit of measure into another. It will be easy to identify these conversion questions on the test, as they contain *units*—in this case, quarts—that appear in ***bold italics***. If the pump can move one gallon every fifteen minutes, how many gallons will it move in an hour? The answer is 4 gallons. Now, the million dollar question: looking at the Reference Sheet, how many quarts are in a gallon? Is that your final answer? Are you sure? The answer is 4 quarts. Therefore, $4 \times 4$ is 16, choice D.

Geometry is a broad category that covers a lot of information, but if you want to narrow your focus a bit, then look at the table below:

**TAAS's Favorite Geometry Categories:**

- measure of angles
- perimeter and area
- questions involving circles and degrees
- triangles, triangles, triangles

Occasionally you'll have a Geometry Question that can be solved just by looking at it, but there are few of those. Still, if you're given a diagram or figure to work with, always try to ballpark the correct answer.

**Strategy**

On Geometry Questions with diagrams, use your eyes if possible to ballpark the correct answer. This can work with both angles and lengths.

7. When the clock is at 4:44, what is the angle between the minute hand and the hour hand?

A. 168 degrees

B. 122 degrees

C. 90 degrees

D. 60 degrees

Since a right angle is 90 degrees, you can simply look at the clock and ask yourself, "Is that angle *greater* or *less than* 90 degrees?" Since the angle on the clock is definitely greater than 90 degrees, you can cross out C, 90 and D, 60, since they're too small. At this point, take a guess, or do the math. B, 122 degrees, is the answer.

While there will be a few relatively straightforward Geometry Questions on the test, most will be a little more esoteric.

8. A triangle has two sides that are 7 cm and 9 cm. Which of the following cannot be the third side?

A. 2 cm

B. 4 cm

C. 7 cm

D. 14 cm

You'll want to know everything there is to know about triangles before you sit down to take the math test, and questions like this are the reason why! Using POE, what can you eliminate? If you said C, then good for you! It's that pesky *Numeralis Eliminatorius* again.

Do you recall how important it is to write everything down? On question 8, try to draw a triangle with sides of 7, 9, and 2 cm. Can you do it (without bending time and space)? Probably not, since you need more than 2 cm to connect 7 cm and 9 cm lines and still have a triangle. Choice A is your answer.

## Strategy

Know all that you can about the TAAS's favorite geometry categories, and be prepared to use that information.

### The Middle Third: Questions 21-44

**TAAS Objective 10:**   Problem Solving Using Estimation
(4 questions)

**TAAS Objective 11:**   Problem Solving Using Solution Strategies
(8 questions)

**TAAS Objective 12:**   Problem Solving Using Mathematical
Representation (8 questions)

**TAAS Objective 13:**   Evaluation of the Reasonableness of a Solution
(4 questions)

The middle third of the Math TAAS is different from the first third in a variety of ways. First, there are now five multiple-choice answers, instead of just four. This increase in the number of possible answers is the best way to realize that you've gone from the first part of the Math TAAS to the second. (The change should occur somewhere around the number 21, depending on the number of field questions.)

This section of the test deals with Objectives 10–13, three of which start with the phrase "Problem Solving Using . . . ." What this means is that you'll see a lot of word problems, so be prepared to do reading. This by itself can cause some difficulty, as you find yourself with about four lines of text filled with numbers, and at the end of the question you have no idea what the question wants. The key here is to realize ahead of time that since many of these questions require more than one step of work, they may take a little more time to solve.

As you think through the solution in your head, write every calculation down.

If you try to work out these problems in your head, you're asking for trouble. Trying to keep track of multiple variables in your head is like juggling with chainsaws: you might be able to get away with it, but if you slip up, the consequences are very painful.

Word problems usually involve the use of *variables*. The plus side of this is that these question are easily recognizable: just look for variables in the question and/or the answer choices. The downside is that POE isn't very effective on this problem type. Ballparking doesn't work on variables, and, since all the answer choices will contain the same numbers as those in the question, you won't be able to eliminate anything based on that criteria. Still, knowing that POE doesn't work here is important, because you will know not to use it.

## Strategy

You can spot a word problem by the presence of variables. To solve this question type, first label what each variable represents.

9. Bernie's Discount Emporium sells four types of lawn chair. The small version is $45, the large version retails for $74, and the deluxe chair is $145. The store sold $t worth of lawn chairs in January. If in January, s represents the number of small lawn chairs sold, l represents the number of large lawn chairs sold, and d the number of deluxe chairs sold, which algebraic equation below represents the money received in January on lawn chair sales?

A. $45s + 74l - 145d = t$

B. $74s + 45l + 145d = t$

C. $45d + 74l = t + 145s$

D. $t = 74l + 145d + 45s$

Lots of writing, lots of variables = problem-solving question. There are four variables in question 9, and if you keep track of what each one represents, you should be able to find the right answer. Going one variable at a time, $s$ stands for the small chairs worth $45, so we can cross out any answer choice that doesn't combine $s$ with 45 (the price of small lawn chairs). That gets rids of B and C, so now it's a fifty-fifty chance between A and D. In both of those choices, each of the variables $s$, $l$, and $d$ is properly aligned with its respective price, but to find the total money received on lawn chair sales, you would add all three variables. In A, the deluxe lawn chair is subtracted, so it's incorrect. That leaves D, your answer.

Go one step at a time, don't get flustered by the extensive writing, keep track of your variables, and problem-solving questions will be at your mercy.

In addition to word problems, the most common question type by far is the Chart/Graph Question. The Middle Third of the Math TAAS is chock full of these visual questions. The easiest form of graph question asks you to interpret basic data correctly. A harder graph question will ask you to read data and then do something with that information. For yet a third type, you'll have to choose the graph that best represents a particular situation.

The graph below shows the amount of money earned by Anju and Jonas while working at a pizzeria.

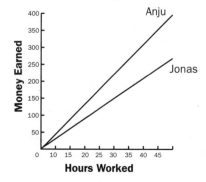

10. Based on the graph, which of the following is true?

    A. Jonas works more hours than Anju each week.

    B. Jonas makes more money per hour then Anju does.

    C. Anju could work fewer hours and still earn as much money as Jonas each week.

    D. Even if Jonas worked the same number of hours as Anju, he can never make the same amount of money she does.

    E. Not here

11. If Anju and Jonas both work 20 hours one week, what is the best estimate of the mean amount of money earned by them?

    A. $300

    B. $200

    C. $150

    D. $100

    E. $50

12. If management decides that Anju will be paid a flat rate of $400 a week, and that Jonas will receive a raise of $1 per hour, then which of the following statements is true?

    A. The slope of Anju's line will be horizontal.

    B. The slope of Jonas's line will decrease.

    C. The slopes of both Jonas's and Anju's lines will increase.

    D. The slope of Anju's line will be vertical.

    E. The slope of Jonas's line will be vertical.

While you probably won't see three graph questions connected to the same graph on the Math TAAS, you might well see two. In any event, the three questions above illustrate three common graph questions. In question 10, you must read the graph correctly. If you do, you should narrow it down to C or D. In the same way that vague, middle-of-the-road answers are better on the reading test, give choice C a good hard look. It contains the broad word *could*, and it's the right answer. Choice D is incorrect if both Anju and Jonas work 0 hours per week.

In question 11, reading the graph is still important, but now you have to combine that with a little number sense terminology. *Mean* stands for average, and the average of their earnings will be the point midway between their two earnings line, straight above 20 hours. Reading across from that point, you get $100, choice D.

For question 12, you have to understand the graph well enough to realize that if Anju receives a flat rate, her payment line won't change in relation to her hours worked. That means her payment line would be a horizontal line coming out of $400. A is your answer.

In order to do well on Graph/Chart Questions, you need to be very comfortable with interpreting data in a visual form. Practice on graphs you find in newspaper, perhaps in the business section. Or you can surf the net, as there are undoubtedly many sites using graphs for information. If you want to move on to the bonus level, construct your own graphs. Graph the number of canned goods in your kitchen, or the number of times the phone rings each week. Go to the nearby mall and make a chart showing how many people will give you a dollar if you ask them politely, or how many people would accompany you to the prom if you asked. With those last two graphs, you'll learn about not only graphs, you'll learn about love and money as well.

*Not learning all you can about graphs and charts for the Math TAAS is a criminal offense.*

There is one last type of question that is often seen in the Middle Third of the test: the Probability Question.

> 13. What are the odds that at least one Probability Question will appear on the Math TAAS?
>
> A. Pretty good
>
> B. About 10 in 25 or 6 to 4
>
> C. No chance at all
>
> D. What are "odds"?
>
> E. I like cake

Hopefully, for question 13, you picked A, Pretty good. There are two types of Probability Question: Either you figure out all the possible combinations, or you figure out the odds of some event occurring. In the first case, the trick is to think *multiplication*.

> 14. The following action figures are sold at a nearby store:

| Soldiers | Dinosaurs | Villains | Superheroes |
|----------|-----------|----------|-------------|
| Capt. Bob | Stegosaurus | Dr. Footlock | Mr. Goodness |
| Audie | Sleestack | Goobertor | Ariadne Jones |
| Sgt. Mekmek | Cerotopus | Skimjeevil | |
| | Dimetrodon | | |

> If you went to the store and bought one of each type of action figure, how many different combinations could be made?
>
> A. 72
>
> B. 36
>
> C. 12
>
> D. 4
>
> E. 2

The phrase *how many different combinations*, or words that mean the same thing, indicate that you've come across the first type of probability question. To solve, list all the different types of action figure, and then *multiply* them together.

3 soldiers x 4 dinosaurs x 3 villains x 2 superheroes =
3  x  4  x  3  x  2  = 72, answer A.

The other type of Probability Question is the *what are the odds* question. For this, you'll need to find two key numbers: The total number of outcomes, and the number of desired outcomes in which a specific event/item will occur. Let's look at an example that's similar to an earlier question.

> 15. A hat contains 90 slips of paper that are either blue, red, or yellow. Half of the slips are yellow, and the ratio of blue slips to red slips is 2 to 1. If one slip is chosen at random, what is the probability that it is red?
>     A. $\frac{1}{2}$
>     B. $\frac{1}{3}$
>     C. $\frac{1}{6}$
>     D. $\frac{1}{12}$
>     E. $\frac{1}{24}$

First, we need the total number of outcomes, which in this case is 90, the number of total slips. Second, we need the specific number of desired outcomes in question, the number of red slips. Half the slips are yellow (45), so that leaves 45 slips remaining. Since blue slips outnumber red slips 2 to 1, there must be 30 blue and 15 red slips. 15 is the second number we're looking for. Now, you must set up a fraction. Place the second number over the first number: $\frac{15}{90}$. This can be reduced to $\frac{1}{6}$, choice C.

## Strategy

On "how many different" combinations questions, think multiplication. On "what are the odds" questions, find the two numbers (total number of outcomes and number of desired outcomes).

### The Final Third: Questions 45–60

**TAAS Objective 6:**   Use of Addition to Solve Problems (4 questions)

**TAAS Objective 7:**   Use of Subtraction to Solve Problems (4 questions)

**TAAS Objective 8:**   Use of Multiplication to Solve Problems (4 questions)

**TAAS Objective 9:**   Use of Division to Solve Problems (4 questions)

Of the three sections on the Math TAAS, the final third might be considered the simplest, since every question centers around whether you can add, subtract, multiply, or divide. As on the middle third, the questions on the final third have five possible answer choices. The fifth answer choice will always be "Not Here." While "Not Here" appears occasionally throughout the middle third, it appears on *every* question in the final third, so it's easy to see when you have entered the last stretch of the math test.

On the final third of the test, if you work through a problem and arrive at a solution that isn't one of the answer choices, you should first recheck your math. If you get the same number again, choose "Not Here" and move on.

"Not Here" is actually the correct answer for a few questions on the final third, so don't be alarmed if you feel you've done the math correctly, but the solution you come up with is nowhere to be found.

Of course, if you get "Not Here" on 7 of the 16 questions throughout the final third, then you have a little problem, because around 4 of those answers are going to be wrong. But hey! At least you know that, and can go over those 7 problems again with a fine-toothed comb.

To do well on the final third of the Math TAAS, keep in mind three main points:

1. Write down all of your work, and don't be sloppy.

2. Use the Formula Chart at the front of the section to help you with any questions requiring conversions.

3. POE works well on questions involving fractions.

Regarding point 1, if a question asks you to add three numbers with decimals, the key will be whether or not you do the math correctly. Don't get sloppy and line up the numbers improperly, and don't be in such a rush that you do the calculations in your head. If you write everything down, you'll be able to spot any mistakes.

As for point 2, some questions are tricky because they're based in irregular units, like the question below.

16. Jaime flew from Anahuac to El Paso, and then from El Paso to Brownsville. The flight from Anahuac to El Paso took 7 hours 45 minutes. The flight from El Paso to Brownsville took 8 hours 55 minutes. What was the total flight time from Anahuac to Brownsville?

   A. 15 hours 40 minutes

   B. 16 hours

   C. 16 hours 30 minutes

   D. 16 hours 40 minutes

   E. Not Here

The trap in this question is the fact that you need to convert the units. Add the two numbers to get 15 hours, 100 minutes. Then, convert this number into 16 hours, 40 minutes.

This example is fairly straightforward, since most people are familiar with converting hours to minutes. But if there's a question converting quarts to ounces, or yards to miles, or cups to gallons, then you might have some trouble. Using the Formula Chart can be an enormous help. Here's another example.

17. A toy store ordered 84 boxes of plastic elves. Each box contained 14 elves. How many elves did the toy store order?

A. 1,176

B. 1,008

C. 840

D. 336

E. Not Here

The primary task for question 17 is to determine if you need to add, subtract, multiply, or divide. Once you decide on a course of action—in this case, multiplication—you multiply 14 (the number of elves per box) by 84 (the number of boxes bought by the store) to find the total number of elves ordered. The answer is . . . a lot of elves! Answer A.

That's all there is to the Math TAAS. Familiarize yourself with the examples listed, but be prepared to improvise on the actual test. Invariably there will be some variations on some questions—a geometry problem combined with fractions, for instance—that can be easily solved if you keep an open mind. In other words, while the questions you see won't be *exactly* like the ones we've discussed, they'll be close enough that the techniques discussed will enable you to find the answer.

However, if you do feel like you're getting in way too deep on a question, just shout "ma*n* dubáu*n*nu!" which means "I'm drowning!" in Nepalese. A lifeguard will come by shortly to rescue you.

# Chapter 4

# WRITING: PART 1

## HOW WRITING: PART 1 IS LIKE TWO DOCTORS HAVING A GOOD PENMANSHIP CONTEST

Oh, when they were young, Dr. Charlene Aybecee and Dr. Markus De E'eff both had great cursive handwriting. Like all children, they made sure to loop their *p*'s and *q*'s properly, and to dot their *i*'s and cross their *t*'s. Their hand-writing was a thing of calligraphic beauty.

But times change. As they grew older, the two doctors started to get a little sloppy. Dr. Aybecee began to rush through her vowels, and her *e* eventually looked little different from her *i*'s and *o*'s. Dr. De E'eff, for his part, got slop-pier and sloppier with his handwriting—until his notes in medical school resembled the scratches made by a horde of chickens running from a farmer's knife.

You may have had a similar experience with grammar. At one point, you understood it, and paid a lot of attention to it. Over time, though, you got a little careless. It didn't matter that your grammar wasn't perfect, because people still understood you. Now, however, you're faced with a test that focuses on your grammar skills. You might feel that you don't know a thing about the subject.

Well, cheer up. Just because Dr. Aybecee and De E'eff didn't maintain their good penmanship doesn't mean they don't know what good penmanship is. Similarly, even if you don't always use perfect grammar, it doesn't mean you can't recognize good grammar when you see it. For that matter, it's just as important to be able to spot *poor* grammar, too. Since part 1 of the Writing TAAS is all multiple-choice, this is all you'll have to concentrate on doing: separate the correct answer choice from the incorrect ones. The strategies in this chapter will help you accomplish this task.

*Don't feel pressured to remember every grammatical rule that there is. A good knowledge of basic sentence structure is all that you'll need on the test.*

## Writing TAAS Format

The Writing TAAS is divided into two parts. Part 1 is a 40-question multiple-choice test covering various grammar, spelling, capitalization, and punctuation rules. Part 2 is an essay, which is discussed in the next chapter.

The scores for Parts 1 and 2 are interdependent; the higher the score on your essay, the lower your score needs to be on the multiple-choice section, and vice versa. The essay is graded on a scale from 1 to 4 (highest). Keep in mind, though, that you must score *at least* a 2 on the essay. So even if you're right on all 40 grammar questions, if your essay gets a 1, you'll have to take the Writing TAAS over again. Beyond an essay score of 1 or 0, the scores are linked in the following way: *The higher the score you receive on the essay, the lower your score needs to be on the 40-question grammar section, and vice versa.*

The following chart shows the breakdown of minimum scores:

| If your essay score is a . . . | . . . then you'll need to get this many questions right on part 1 |
|:---:|:---:|
| 4 | $\frac{6}{40}$ |
| 3 | $\frac{16}{40}$ |
| 2 | $\frac{26}{40}$ |

In other words, if you receive a 4 on your essay, then you'll need to get just 6 of the 40 grammar questions right. If you score a 3 on the essay, then you'll need to get 16 questions right.

Sadly, the one problem with this linked-score system is that you don't get to find out your grammar score *before* you have to write the essay. You'll have no idea how well you fared on either section until the test is over. So be sure to give each section all your effort.

## Strategy

Since you won't be able to gauge your scores beforehand, try not to focus on the linked-scoring system. Do your best on each section, independent of the other. Aim for at least a 26 on grammar and a 2 on the essay, and you'll have the best chance of passing.

Another way to think of the scoring breakdown is to recognize that you'll have to get about 65 percent of the grammar questions right. You won't have to agonize over any single question, since you can still miss 14 questions and get a passing score. Perfection is always a wonderful thing to behold, but it's not needed to get a healthy score on the Writing TAAS.

## Writing TAAS: Part 1

Part 1 is divided into three sections. Each section tests a different TAAS Writing Objective, and each has a different question format. Following is how the question numbers relate to the TAAS Objectives.

| | |
|---|---|
| **Writing Questions 1–12:** | TAAS Objective 6, *English Usage* |
| **Writing Questions 13–26:** | TAAS Objective 5, *Sentence Construction* |
| **Writing Questions 27–40:** | TAAS Objective 7, *Spelling, Capitalization, and Punctuation* |

You might be wondering why the TEA didn't start with objectives numbered 1, 2, and 3. In fact, objectives 1–4 deal with the *essay* part of the test, and objectives 5–7 deal with the *grammar* part being discussed here. And the numbers are out of order because questions 1–12 deal with Objective 6, questions 13–26 deal with Objective 5, etcetera. While the objective numbers are a bit confusing, when you receive your writing scores back, they'll detail how many Objective 5 questions you got right, how many Objective 6 questions you got right, and so forth. The information is listed here so that you'll know *which* objectives relate to *which* questions.

Now that you know there are three sections with three question types, you won't be bothered when the question format suddenly changes.

## The First Third: Questions 1–12

### TAAS Objective 6: *English Usage*

For the most part, questions 1–12 are fill-in-the-blank questions. There will be two boxed-in passages containing 6–10 related sentences; six of them will be missing key verbs, pronouns, adjectives, and adverbs. Here's an example.

Some people _____(1)_____ that scientists have discovered all of the world's animal species, but this isn't the case. In fact, new species _____(2)_____ almost every month. Many of these discoveries take place in tropical rainforests around the world, partially because rainforests usually contain a huge variety of plant and animal life.

However, new animal species _____(3)_____ to just the rainforests. Some new forms of life are found in some of the _____(4)_____ places on Earth. The bottom of the ocean, for instance, was once thought to be _____(5)_____ empty of life, but expeditions have found unique worms and other animals living next to deep-sea vents.

1. A. believe
   B. believing
   C. will believe
   D. are believing

2. A. will be discovered
   B. are discovered
   C. had been discovered
   D. discovered

3. A. are not hardly limited
   B. aren't never limited
   C. are not limited
   D. are not barely limited

4.  A. most inaccessible

    B. inaccessible

    C. more inaccessiblest

    D. most inaccessibler

5.  A. largely

    B. largest

    C. larger

    D. large

The best piece of advice you can take into the usage section, as well as into the entire multiple-choice section, is to look for an answer choice that has *few words*. Let's be honest about the English language. While it does have many different verb tenses, the ones we use the most are *past, present*, and *future*. The most frequent answer choices on the Writing TAAS contain one of the three most common tenses. The other tenses—those that have the added words *been, have*, and *are*—are often misleading answer choices.

## Strategy

In general, the fewer words in the answer choice (in the form of past, present, or future verb form), the better.

If you're wondering why this is the case, just remember that while most people speak English fairly well and with ease, they don't necessarily all believe that they know "proper grammar." It's as if the word "grammar" conjures up an image of frighteningly difficult rules, and the human brain just shuts off. If you approached the Writing TAAS with that idea, your eye would be drawn to choices C and D in question 1. Thinking that the fundamentals of English are complex, you might incorrectly conclude that the answer should be complex as well. Actually, the *opposite* is true more often than not on the Writing TAAS. On question 1, the answer is the *present tense*, choice A.

While you *do* want to narrow in on answer choices with the most common verb tenses, you *don't* want to simply pick the one that has the shortest/fewest words. That would be too simplistic. Instead, try using the "less is more" principle to *eliminate wrong answers*, rather than to select a right answer. Look at question 2. If you choose the shortest answer, you would pick D, which is wrong. On the other hand, if you rule out unlikely

> Roughly 6–9 usage questions will require that you select the proper verb form. The *past* and *present* tenses are by far the most common right answers on the test.

answers following the "less is more" rule, you would get the long answer choices, A and C, out of the way. That would leave B and D, both of which are well-used tenses, present and past. In this case, B is the answer.

There's almost sure to be a question that deals with double negatives, as in question 3. You may recall that two wrongs don't make a right, and in grammar two negative words together—a double negative—don't make a correct sentence. For this type of question, you can safely eliminate any answer choice that contains **two** or more of the following words: *not, never, hardly, never, scarcely, barely,* and the contraction *n't.*

### Strategy

A sentence should contain only one negative word at a time. If an answer choice contains two of the following words, it can't be correct: *not, never, hardly, never, scarcely, barely,* and the contraction *n't.*

These are all negative words, and you don't need more than one of them in a sentence. Look at question 3 and apply this technique; you'll find that you're left with only one choice, C. Pretty neat, eh? You could have answered this question correctly without even looking at the passage.

> ## Strategy
>
> Before reading a passage, look through the answer choices and eliminate any choices that you know contain imaginary words or improper grammar.

One way to take control of the test is to jump ahead to the questions *before* you read a passage, so you can rule out any clearly incorrect answer choices. If you can cross out any choices with improper grammar or made-up words even before attempting a question, your odds will be better! While other students are slogging through the passage, you'll be answering questions, which is all that really counts.

This technique works well on questions 3 and 4. On question 3, choices A, B, and D all contain improper grammar. On question 4, choices C and D can be ruled out, because *inaccessiblest* and *inaccessibler* are made up words.

> Sounding out a sentence in your head is helpful. The answer that seems right to your ear is usually the correct choice.

While you'll find these tips useful on many questions, you will have to know some basics of English grammar. On question 5, for example, all of the answer choices are grammatically correct. If you're unsure of the solution, try speaking the sentence to yourself and see what "sounds" right.

Even if you're unsure about your grammar usage, you probably know more than you think. On question 5, sound out the answer choices. The one that should seem best to you is the adverb *largely*, choice A. But if you thought all of them sounded okay, with the exception of *large*, which sounds very awkward in the sentence, you could also cross out D and then guess.

One last point about usage questions on the Writing test: Did you read the entire passage from start to finish, including the sentences that had no questions (no identifying numbers) attached to them? If you did, then answer this question: What's helpful about reading a sentence that doesn't have a question attached to it? Answer: Nothing! Read only those sentences that have questions attached to them. Occasionally, you might have to read a nonquestion sentence in order to get the context of something, but for the most part, focus on only those sentences that are identified with questions.

## Strategy

While reading an entire passage is useful on the Reading TAAS, the *opposite* is true on Writing. Here, read only the sentences that have questions attached to them. Your goal is to answer very pointed grammar/spelling questions, so even if you find a passage fascinating to read, don't take the time to do so.

Your primary task for Writing: Part 1 is to answer questions about *spelling, grammar,* and *sentence construction.* You won't need to know the main idea of a passage or the emotional state of a character as you will on the Reading TAAS. You see, if you spend time reading all the filler sentences, you'll likely fall into the *reading for overall understanding* mode. And if you do that, you'll be less likely to notice specific grammar mistakes. In other words, if you're busy reading for the main idea, you won't focus on punctuation or spelling—they require different types of concentration.

### The Middle Third: Questions 13–26

### TAAS Objective 5: *Sentence Construction*

The Sentence Construction section will have four boxed-in passages followed by a total of 14 questions. Look at the sample passage below.

> (6) Lisa left her room when her mother called her downstairs. She left her room carrying her gym bag. Lisa was excited about competing in the state judo tournament. (7) She ran outside, jumped in the car with her parents, forgetting to lock the front door. The excitement of the tournament was all she could think about. (8) When her brother reminded her of the unlocked door, Lisa was embarrassed. She stepped out of the car and closed the front door carefully. "All right!," she screamed when she returned to the car, "Anyone in this family who doesn't cheer for me today is going to get hurt!"

6. A. Lisa left her room, when her mother called her downstairs she left her room carrying her gym bag.

    B. Carrying her gym bag, Lisa left her room when her mother called her downstairs.

    C. Lisa left her room, carrying her gym bag, when her mother called her downstairs.

    D. Carrying her gym bag, her mother called her downstairs and Lisa left her room.

7. A. Forgetting to lock the front door, she ran outside and jumped in the car with her parents.

    B. Jumping in the car with her parents, she ran outside forgetting to lock the front door.

    C. She ran outside. She jumped in the car with her parents, she forgot to lock the front door.

    D. Correct as is.

8. A. When her brother reminded her of the unlocked door, and Lisa was embarrassed.

    B. Lisa, embarrassed, when her brother reminded of the unlocked door.

    C. When her brother, reminded her of the unlocked door. Lisa was embarrassed.

    D. Correct as is.

All right, first things first: Did you spend the time reading the last two sentences, in which Lisa screams at her family? If you didn't, good for you, as it was thrown in just to test whether you would read unnecessary sentences.

The key to this section is sentence construction. Is the underlined text the best way to state something? Before you ask yourself that question, however, look at the answer choices to see if there is a "Correct as is" answer. If there *isn't*, then the question must have a flaw in it.

## Strategy

For Sentence Construction questions, first see whether one of the answer choices is "Correct as is." If it's not there, then the question must have a flaw in it.

Look at question 6. The answer choices are all different from the sentence in the text; therefore, you know that the underlined part of question 6 is wrong. Another way to tell that the underlined phrase is wrong is by seeing that the phrase "left her room" is repeated twice. Clearly, this sentence is poorly constructed.

A repeated phrase doesn't necessarily mean that a sentence is grammatically wrong. It might just mean that the sentence would be clearer and more effective if it were written another way.

> Look for *repeated phrases* within an underlined section. They almost always mean the sentence needs to be rewritten.

**Items to focus on:**

1. Replace repeated phrases with the proper pronouns.
2. Replace repeated phrases by combining sentences.
   (to eliminate repetition)
3. Use transitions correctly (conjunctions like *and*, *or* and *but*, as well as commas).

On question 6, item 2 works best. You can eliminate the repeated phrase by combining the two sentences. Since choice A doesn't eliminate the repetition, it should be crossed out. That leaves B, C, and D. Read them carefully to determine exactly *who* is carrying the gym bag in each. In choice D, Lisa's mother is carrying it, and in C, the room seems to be carrying the bag. That's quite a room, but not a good answer. The correct choice is B.

On question 7, the key is to use better transitions. Choice C repeats the pronoun "she" too many times for it to be correct. Choice A, on the other hand, places the three events in the proper sequence, and in one neat, tidy sentence. A is the way to go here.

> The TEA has provided some clues about the questions on this section. One clue is to look for "correctly written sentences that need to be combined [question 6], as well as run-on sentences [question 7]."

There are no errors in sentence 8, so the answer is choice D. Keep in mind that 2 or 3 questions in this section won't have any errors. If you end up with "Correct as is" as your answer six times, you'll know that's too often. On the other hand, if you never select "Correct as is," you're being a little too gung-ho about finding faults.

### The Final Third: Questions 27–40

**TAAS Objective 7:** *Spelling, Capitalization, and Punctuation*

The final third of Writing: Part 1 will contain three boxed-in passages, followed by a total of 14 questions.

Although it took over twenty hours, the hiking party (9) finally entered Mount Rainier National park. They were all eager to start climbing the mountain, but since it was late in the day they decided to camp out and wait until morning. While waiting, the hiking party made (10) sure they had all the food, equipment and clothing they would need for the trek.

The next (11) morning, the party started towards the summit. The weather was (12) excelent for hiking, with clear skies for miles around. Everyone was enjoying themselves immensely . . . until the bears came.

9.  A. Spelling error

    B. Capitalization error

    C. Punctuation error

    D. No error

10. A. Spelling error

    B. Capitalization error

    C. Punctuation error

    D. No error

11. A. Spelling error

    B. Capitalization error

    C. Punctuation error

    D. No error

12. A. Spelling error

    B. Capitalization error

    C. Punctuation error

    D. No error

As you can see, all the answer choices are the same in this section. The approach to every problem is also the same.

## Strategy

The best way to approach these questions is to start with choice A and check for a spelling error. If you don't find one, look for a capitalization error (B). If you don't find one, look for a punctuation error (C). If you don't find one, pick D.

Spelling errors should be the easiest to spot. You just look at the word, and based on your knowledge of spelling, you will know if there is a mistake.

Then, look for capitalization errors, which are a little harder. For these, you have to make a distinction about how the word is used in the sentence. For example, "I asked my father if I could go to the store," is not the same as "I asked Father McSwirly if I could go to the store." The second sentence refers to a proper noun (a specific person), so both words need to be capitalized.

If there are no spelling or capitalization errors in a sentence, try looking for punctuation errors next. Punctuation errors are the hardest to spot, since you have to concentrate on the structure of the sentence. On the TAAS, about half of the punctuation errors involve *commas*.

If you've looked for the three types of errors and you haven't found any, then the answer must be D, No error. Once again, bear in mind that 2 or 3 of the 14 questions won't have any errors, so make sure you don't have too many or too few "No error" answers in the section.

Using the technique described above, look at question 9. It doesn't appear to have any spelling errors, so A can be crossed out. However, *park* is referring to a specific place, Mount Rainier National Park, so it should be capitalized. At this point, you can pick B and move on.

Question 10 at first glance has no spelling or capitalization errors. It does, however, need a comma after *equipment*, since this is part of a list that needs to be set off. For question 11, you should come up empty when you check for spelling, capitalization, and punctuation. That's fine, since the answer is D. And for question 12, *excellent* is missing a consonant (an extra l), so A is the answer. In fact, the most common form of spelling error on this section of the Writing TAAS is a *missing letter*, so be on the lookout for that.

# Chapter 5

# WRITING: PART 2

## HOW THE TAAS WRITING PROMPT IS LIKE A STICK OF BUBBLE GUM

By itself, a stick of bubble gum isn't very interesting. It's nothing more than a flat, strangely colored rectangle made out of a substance that looks a lot like cardboard. But once you place the gum in your mouth, everything starts to change. First, you get a burst of flavor, and as your jaw muscles start flexing, the gum takes on an ever-changing variety of shapes. Place it between your lips, exhale, and the flat stick of gum has transformed into a bubblegum bubble.

Similarly, the Writing TAAS is nothing more than a string of words. It's up to you to take the prompt and use it to create a concise, insightful essay that will earn you a high score on this part of the test. To do this you'll have to read the prompt, flex your mental muscles to come up with the key ingredients for your composition, and then exhale those words onto paper. The end result should be an essay that is as contained and logical as a sphere of chewing gum.

*A solitary student walks the moors reviewing for the Writing TAAS.*

Although you're probably well-versed with the basics of essay writing, this chapter will review what's expected of you on the Writing TAAS.

### Writing TAAS: Part 2

The essay is graded on a scale of 1–4. You must get at least a score of 2 to pass the test. Listed below is a brief description of each score, as well as a recap of how many of the part 1 multiple-choice questions you'll need to answer correctly.

| If your essay score is a . . . | . . . then you'll need to get this many questions right on part 1 |
|---|---|
| 4 (High) | $\frac{6}{40}$ |
| 3 (Passing) | $\frac{16}{40}$ |
| 2 (Minimum Passing) | $\frac{26}{40}$ |
| 1 (Failing) | N/A |
| 0 (Unscorable) | N/A |

A score of 0 means that the essay was incomprehensible or way off topic, such as when you've been asked to write an essay about traffic rules but instead you write a fiery letter to the Mayor of Houston demanding that he stop trying to read your thoughts through your aluminum-foil helmet.

On the day of the test, the schedule should run as follows:

1.  Students arrive and sit down in desks.
2.  Students plead with administrator in charge to let them not take the test.
3.  Administrator either:
    a) says "No"
    b) does not dignify statement with a response
4.  Students receive a writing prompt. This will either be a persuasive or informative prompt.
5.  Students now have time to write their essays. Only the completed essay, and not any notes, will be graded.

The methods used to score your essay provide interesting insight on how to approach it. Your essay will be graded by two readers, each of whom assigns it between 0–4 points. If the two graders disagree on your score, a third grader will be brought in to act as a tiebreaker. The readers (primarily Texas teachers) award the score based on the following objectives:

| *Writing TAAS Objective* | *What it Means* |
|---|---|
| *1. Focus* | How well does the essay present and maintain a clear theme or idea? |
| *2. Organization* | Is there a coherent structure to the development of the essay, such as a beginning, middle, and end? Are transitional devices used properly? Is there a conclusion? |
| *3. Conventions* | Does the essay have proper punctuation, spelling, capitalization, and variation in sentence structure? |
| *4. Support* | What is the quality of the details used to support the main idea? Are the details credible, thorough, and elaborate? |

Hypothetically, if you write a deeply moving essay with atrocious grammar, you might still get a 2, which is the minimum passing score. This is because 75 percent of the objectives have to do with *content*, not grammar. On the other hand, if you write an absolutely bland, disorganized essay with perfect grammar, you might not get 2 points, assuming it lacks focus, organization, and support. With this in mind, concentrate on developing effective content, and worry less about using perfect grammar.

## Strategy

When planning your essay, concentrate on developing the content and transitions more than on using perfect spelling and grammar. Those are things you can always check later.

You can always go through your essay before time runs out and check your spelling and grammar. But it's much harder to repair an essay that hasn't been developed well from the start. Spend your energy on writing a clear, well-supported essay that holds together well or your score will suffer.

Although content is awarded more than grammar, your essay still must be comprehensible. A sentence so jumbled that it makes no sense won't help you at all, since the reader won't be able to understand your point. Consider the following three sentences.

A. I believe students should be allowed to vote in national elections.
B. I believe the students they should be aloud to vote national elections.
C. I believe the students they vote and national elections.

Sentence A has good grammar and clear content. Sentence B has some misspellings and incorrect grammar, but the writer still makes his point. Sentence C, however, is grammatically incorrect and unclear. Shoot to write the best sentence possible (Sentence A), but if you have to settle for a slightly imperfect one (Sentence B), bear in mind that topic development is worth more than conventions.

### Writing Prompt

For the essay, you'll be given a writing prompt (an assignment/topic) about which to write. The prompt will be either an informative prompt or a persuasive prompt. An *informative* prompt asks you to explain a topic or describe a concept, while a *persuasive* prompt asks you to convince the reader of a certain point of view. Since the prompts require you to do different things, the first thing you should do on this essay is to determine what kind of essay you'll need to write. Will you have to convey information, or will you have to persuade?

This isn't very hard to do. Informative prompts often have the word "explain" in them, while persuasive prompts often contain the phrase "your point of view." Both require you to use specific examples and information to make your essay clear, detailed and convincing.

### Examples of Informative and Persuasive Prompts

Informative Prompts:

- Think of a job you would like to do. Now explain why you would like to do that job.
- Think of all the places in the world. Pick your favorite place and explain why you like it so much.

Persuasive Prompts:

- Write a letter to convince your parents to accept your point of view on the effect watching TV has on grades.
- Many adults think that having a curfew helps prevents crime. Write an essay on whether or not you believe a curfew is an effective deterrent to crime.

### Time to Flex your Mental Muscles

After reading the prompt, you should begin to plan what you will write. There's a lot of time, so don't feel pressured to start writing immediately.

> **Strategy**
>
> Give yourself 10–15 minutes to brainstorm as many ideas as possible. Write them all down, making brief notes about how each one relates to your main idea.

The key to good brainstorming is to draw some conclusions on your own, using the text to back up your ideas. To illustrate this idea, look at the following writing prompt again.

- Many adults think that having a curfew helps prevents crime. Write an essay on whether or not you believe a curfew is an effective deterrent to crime.

First, you'll have to decide if you want to argue that curfews are (or aren't) an effective deterrent to crime. It doesn't matter what side you take; all that matters is how *well* you support your main idea. As the writing prompt indicates, the emphasis is on how convincing you are, and whether your supporting details are concrete and valid. After all, your opinions must be *based* on something, and it's up to you to explain what that "something" is. There's no correct answer, only a well-supported argument versus a poorly supported argument.

## Strategy

After you read a persuasive prompt, decide which side of the argument you'll support. For an informative prompt, decide on what topic you want to explain.

Let's say you're writing a persuasive essay that states curfews are an effective deterrent to crime. So that you can practice, take the time now to brainstorm as many ideas as possible that will help support this statement. Do this on your own, and then compare it to the list below.

**Brainstorming Ideas for the Pro-Curfew Persuasive Essay**

1. Most crimes occur at night, so having a curfew would limit criminals' ability to get around.

2. Random crimes of opportunity—like breaking a car window to get to some CD's—should decrease.

3. Police would have an easier time preventing crime. (few people out at night)

4. Infringement on people's freedom not total (still a lot of time to roam streets).

5. A one-year study could be done to see if the curfew actually deterred crime.

6. Human-Eating Robots come out most often at night—curfew would help prevent crimes of digestion.

> Don't plan your essay on the two lined pages provided in the test booklet, since that space is needed for the essay and nothing else. Use the separate sheet provided for your notes.

As you can see from idea 6, some thoughts aren't as good as others. But don't sweat it; the whole point of brainstorming is to come up with as many ideas as possible, with no obligation to use all of them.

**Pacing Suggestions: Essay**

| | |
|---|---|
| Brainstorm | 10 minutes |
| Organize | 10 minutes |
| Write essay | 20 minutes |
| Proofread | 5 minutes |

After you finish brainstorming, take some time to organize and elaborate on your thoughts. This is where you'll decide which ideas you'll use and what order they'll go in. You'll consider how to use transitions from one idea to the next. You'll make sure that you introduce your essay (stating the main idea,) then go in to the body of the text where you present your supporting details, and finally, conclude with an idea that restates (in different words) the main idea that you started with. The goal of the organization stage is to get a good sense of what your essay is going to look like. You may want to set up an informal outline to help make sure you've included the essential components.

To return to the bubble gum analogy, if brainstorming is like chewing the gum, then organizing and developing the essay is like lining up the gum between your lips in order to make the bubble. It's an important stage: If you place the gum in the wrong place, your bubble pops before it ever gets big. If you don't organize your thoughts well, your essay won't reach the level of detail and clarity needed to get a high mark.

### Details, Details, Details

Precise, elaborate details are crucial to any essay. To illustrate the importance of details, read the following sentences which range from *vague* to *elaborately detailed*.

1. There is a cat.
2. There is a large cat over there.
3. There is a large cat coming toward you.
4. There is a tiger running at you.

5.  There is a vicious, five-hundred pound tiger named Glorkon running rapidly toward you. He just escaped from the circus, and he is very tired of having chairs stuck in his face.

As you can see, providing sufficient details can mean the difference between *staying alive* and *becoming tiger chow.*

Luckily, the Writing TAAS is not so high-stakes that you have to write a perfectly concise and compelling essay. However, you should make it a point to *elaborate on* and *connect* all of your ideas. Don't assume anything on the part of the reader. For instance, take the statement *Random crimes of opportunity—like breaking a car window to get to some CD's—should decrease.* This statement shouldn't be written down and forgotten. Instead, add to it, by writing something like the following:

> With a curfew, many random crimes of opportunity should decrease. Many times teenagers, who commit a fair amount of vandalism and petty theft, are simply bored. They walk around the neighborhood looking for something to do, and often end up doing foolish and criminal things, like breaking a car window to get to some CD's, just for a cheap thrill. However, with a curfew in place, teenagers wouldn't be as likely to go out, and if they did, they would have to be more cautious about their activities. While having bored teenagers stay indoors could lead to an increase in prank phone calls, at least property damage would decrease.

### The Opposing Argument

When you write a persuasive essay, you should remember that there's always another valid viewpoint. The fact that you chose the *pro*-curfew side doesn't mean that the *anti*-curfew side is *completely wrong.* So put away your pro-curfew posters, cancel the pro-curfew rally you planned, and think about what arguments or reasons would be included in an anti-curfew essay. Include a few of those in your essay, along with an explanation of why they aren't "valid." That way, you'll have presented a *complete* argument, not just your opinion on something.

## Strategy

Try to present an understanding of *both sides* of an argument. If you can describe, and then counter, the other side's position, your essay will be more complete.

Look at brainstorm items 4 and 5. They both attempt to see the anti-curfew side of things, and then go on to counter those arguments. Your essay could include the following paragraph.

> There are people who will argue that a curfew is unconstitutional because it infringes on their freedom. While this is a valid concern, there are steps that could be taken to limit this argument. First, the curfew could be set late, for instance, from midnight to 6:00 A.M., so that most people would not even notice or mind its existence. Second, the curfew could be a temporary one, say for only one year, to judge whether it is an effective deterrent. If it turned out not to be, or if it stopped only a small percentage of crime, then the policy could be abandoned. But if it led to a large decrease in criminal activity, which is very possible, then most people would want to keep the curfew in place.

As you can see, the paragraph above takes the opposition's argument and counters it. While you shouldn't spend the entire essay attacking your opponent's position, one paragraph on the subject is a very good idea.

### Hey Mumbles! Be Sure to Write Neatly

If your cursive handwriting is so bad that sometimes even you don't know what you've written, make sure to print out your essay. Graders cannot grade what they cannot read, and it would be a tragedy if a well-written essay lost points because it couldn't be read.

## Strategy

Make sure you read over your essay and correct any errors in grammar, punctuation, or sentence construction.

Before you hand in your essay, make sure you allow some time to review it. Look it over for any awkwardness or errors. Your essay should *flow* from one idea to the next, and the link between the ideas should be explained. Assume that the reader will know nothing about your topic, and make sure to include all the components of an effective essay. If you need to make any corrections, do so neatly.

Once you have finished proofreading your essay, you're done. Now that the Writing TAAS is under your belt, there's nothing to do but kick back, relax, and maybe . . . chew some gum.

# Chapter 6

# SCIENCE

## HOW THE TAAS SCIENCE TEST IS LIKE
## THE KREBS CYCLE AND RIDING A BICYCLE

Imagine Person A and Person B are sitting on a couch one Saturday after-noon. They both have the option of either staying where they are and watch-ing *World's Best Bowling Mistakes* for the third time or going outside for a bike ride. Person A decides to go for a nice five-mile spin around the neigh-borhood, but Person B opts to stay on the couch and watch that one scene where the person accidentally eats the ten pin, confusing it for an oblong sourdough sandwich.

Based on this information, who do you think will use more energy and burn more calories, Person A, riding a bike, or Person B, sitting on the couch? Most of you would guess A, and that's right, since everyone knows that phys-ical labor takes more energy than being a couch potato. It's just common sense. Now, here's the bonus question: What is the Krebs cycle, and how would riding a bike affect it?

That question is a little tougher to answer, so here's some help. The Krebs cycle is the name for a chemical reaction in the human body that converts food into energy. So riding a bike would cause an increase in the Krebs cycle since more energy is needed for that activity. This explanation is fine and dandy, but here's the most important point: You didn't need to know a thing about the Krebs cycle in order to know that Person A used more energy than Person B.

## Strategy

On the Science TAAS, you don't need to know the exact scientific terms in order to understand how something works.

To put it another way, common sense is often all you need to answer a multiple-choice question on the Science TAAS. For instance, you didn't need to know what the Krebs cycle was to know that riding a bike uses more energy than sitting on a couch. So don't think that you have to be Einstein in order to succeed on this section of the test. Sure, being Einstein would help, but you can still score well if you think of yourself as Einstein's little brother or sister, who doesn't know all the proper scientific terms but has a lot of common sense.

*Using the Krebs cycle, a man rides through town.*

## Science TAAS Breakdown

The Science TAAS is like the other TAAS subject tests, and you probably have a good idea of what that means by now. It consists of 40 multiple-choice questions designed to test five TAAS Objectives. The table below provides an interesting look at what subjects it is designed to cover:

| TAAS Objective | Number of Questions on Science TAAS |
|---|---|
| 1. Scientific Inquiry, Inference, and Communication | 8 |
| 2. Critical Thinking and Problem Solving | 8 |
| 3. Living System Interdependency/Genetic Change | 8 |
| 4. Characteristics of the Universe/Matter and Energy | 8 |
| 5. Earth Systems/Natural Events and Human Activities | 8 |
| **Total Number of Questions** | 40 |
| **Minimum Number of Correct Answers Needed to Pass** | 30 |

While the Science TAAS is set up like its Math, Reading, and Writing siblings, there's one important difference. While those other three tests are given to students at various grades, the Science and Social Studies tests are currently given in grade 8 only. And since they're so new, they currently do not affect your 'advancement' status.

In other words, don't worry about these two TAAS tests as much as you do the Math, Reading, and Writing tests. Granted, they're important, but a low Science score won't keep you from grade 9. The same can't always be said for Math, Reading, and Writing. These three tests are typically used to determine grade promotion.

The Science and Social Studies tests are not currently used to determine whether you can advance to the next grade.

That takes some of the pressure off, doesn't it? Study the skills in this chapter and improve your Science TAAS score, and do so without anxiety.

## The Moderately Sized Three Question Types—Science Style

Granted, there are five different types of multiple-choice questions on the Science TAAS, but this exam is not the same as its Reading, Writing, and Math predecessors. The simple reason is that the subjects tested in science are much broader than in math and English Language Arts. For instance, the Math TAAS tests geometry, but it concentrates on a select range of topics— area, angles, triangles—within that category. On the Science TAAS, the range of topics in the Earth Systems/Natural Events & Human Activities is much broader, ranging from gravity to erosion to volcanoes to the tides. Because of the broad range of topics, and because the topics tested change significantly from year to year, categorizing Earth Systems/Natural Events & Human Activities as a content strand wouldn't help you much.

But don't despair! This just means that the Science test is a little different from the Reading and Math tests. Learn the following techniques and you'll be better prepared than most for this section.

### 1. Common Sense/POE Questions

Never underestimate the amount of scientific knowledge you actually know.

1.  Temperature and _____ are two primary factors that determine the brightness of a star as seen from Earth.

    A. density

    B. radioactivity

    C. distance

    D. water content

Scan the answer choices and ask yourself, "If there is a light far away, what would affect how bright it is?" Choices A, density, and B, radioactivity, are nice scientific terms, but how would they affect the brightness of a light? Imagine a person is holding a lantern 100 feet from you. What would make the light brighter? If that person moved 50 feet closer, wouldn't the light be brighter?

If you think the answer is yes, then you're right. The answer is C, distance.

Common sense can be applied to many Science questions. It often helps to restate the problem into simpler terms. Changing a question about the brightness of a star billions of miles away into one about a lantern being held nearby makes it much easier.

2. Heat absorbed by the earth during the day is radiated into space at night and cools the earth's surface. This cooling is **least** likely to occur on a night when it is

A. clear and dry.

B. windy and rainy.

C. cloudy and calm.

D. cloudy and windy.

Even if you're not an expert at radiational cooling, you still have at least a one in four chance of getting this question right, and a little POE could help those odds even more. Ask yourself, "Which factors would help keep heat in the earth? When I'm outside, does a breeze help cool me off?" Of course it does, which is why you can eliminate B and D. The earth would probably be cooled off by winds in the same manner that you are cooled off. That leaves A and C, so take a guess. If you feel that clouds and a lack of moving air would help keep heat in, choice C, you'll be right.

## Strategy

Try mixing the scientific property know as "common sense" with POE in a 1:1 ratio. It's a sure formula for success!

### 2. Visual Information Questions

A picture is worth a thousand words. It's also worth a lot of points on the Science TAAS, since over half of the questions will have a visual component. This might be a map, a chart, a graph, or some other type of picture.

Bucket 1     Bucket 2     Bucket 3     Bucket 4

3.  The four buckets above contain samples of sand, silt, and
    pebbles. Which bucket shows the most likely settling pat-
    tern for the contents?

    A.  Bucket 1

    B.  Bucket 2

    C.  Bucket 3

    D.  Bucket 4

One thing's for certain: You wouldn't want to drink the contents of any of
the buckets. Beyond that, which of the three objects—sand, silt, or pebbles—
is heaviest? It stands to reason that the heaviest particles will settle at the bottom, while the lightest will go to the top. Since pebbles are the heaviest, eliminate any choices that don't have pebbles at the bottom. C is your answer.

Use the topographic map to answer question 4.

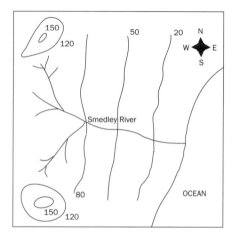

4. The Smedley River flows in what direction?
   A. North

   B. South

   C. East

   D. West

You don't need to be a riverologist—or whatever you call someone who knows about rivers—in order to answer this. Since the Smedley River crosses the map in a fairly horizontal straight line, you can first eliminate choices A and B, North and South. Just by looking you can see that the river isn't going in either of these directions. At this point, you could either guess or look at the elevation numbers on the map. The higher numbers are on the left side of the page, and since you know waters flow downhill, C is the correct answer.

Another way to come up with choice C using common sense is to realize that rivers always flow into the ocean, not the other way around.

## Strategy

When a question is accompanied by a graph/picture, the answer can always be found there. The picture isn't included just for fun; rather, it's the key to finding the answer.

While these questions will ask you about some scientific topic, properly deciphering the visual information will be the most important task. This is good news, since it means that a graph question about aqueous solutions is primarily just a graph question. It would be possible to get a question like this question right if you're good with graphs, regardless of how knowledgeable you are about aqueous solutions. Your expertise in a test-taking strategy (reading graphs and deciphering visual information) can help you overcome a deficiency in your scientific knowledge.

### 3. Jargon Questions

Many questions on the test will test your knowledge of science and scientific terms.

> 5. Which of the following gas(es) is **not** the result of natural processes?
>     A. carbon dioxide
>
>     B. ozone
>
>     C. glucose
>
>     D. chlorofluorcarbons

Have you ever heard people talking about the *ozone layer*? If so, you might guess it wasn't produced by humans. In fact, it's an atmospheric layer which blocks most solar ultraviolet radiation from entering the lower atmosphere. So choice D, chlorofluorocarbons, must be the answer.

Even if you don't know the precise answer for question 5, the extent to which you know scientific terms can help you use POE. For instance, you might look at the answer choices and realize that choice C isn't even a gas, so it won't be the answer. When you exhale (a natural process!), you breathe out carbon dioxide, a fact many of you know, so that means A can't be correct. That leaves B or D, so take a guess.

As you can see, the more you know about scientific terms, the better your chances of doing well; so brush up as much as you can. Even though the range of science topics that appears on the test is quite broad, there are some recurring themes you would do well to review.

### Science TAAS Favorites

1. Basic Genetics: What are dominant and recessive genes, and how do they combine?

2. Basic Knowledge about Elements: Simple formulas about how elements combine, and general information about metals, gases, and liquids.

3. The Food and Water Cycles: Basic information about the food chain, from plants to the big predators, and basic knowledge about how storms, rain, rivers, and oceans are all connected.

4. Current Environmental Issues: Current topics such as the greenhouse effect, E. coli in contaminated water supplies, and the loss of natural habitats and rainforest conservation.

While these are large topics, you'll be in good shape if you go in knowing their big picture components (the basics!), as well as their important terms. You won't need to know the finer details and complex scientific breakdowns. You should be able to get through most of the questions using common sense and a general knowledge of the topics above. Of course, some questions won't have any visual information, and they won't be very susceptible to POE, but these questions will be tough for all students, not just you. So don't panic if you can't figure out a problem. Leave it for the second pass, and then take your best shot.

When the testing day is over, go out and blow off some steam by going for a bike ride. Tell your parents you're going out "to convert some acetyl groups into adenosine triphosphate and guanosinetriphosphate but that they shouldn't worry because you promise not to lose any oxaloacetate." Then, rush out the door before they recover from shock.

# Chapter 7

# SOCIAL STUDIES

## HOW HISTORY ON THE TAAS IS LIKE DRAWING A RAINBOW USING EITHER A 16-, 64-, OR 128-PIECE BOX OF CRAYONS

When it comes to drawing rainbows with crayons, there's a world of difference between the 16- and 128-piece sets. With the 16-piece set, that shift from yellow to green is hard, and the transition from indigo to violet is almost impossible to pull off. Sure, you can draw a rainbow, but it might not even stay two months on the family fridge.

On the other hand, a 128-piece set allows you to draw an incredibly exact rainbow, with subtle shading throughout. You'll have some colors, like Wackberry Blue and Nonchalant Pumpkin, that you won't even know what to do with. A rainbow drawn with that many colors will stay on the fridge for a long time, and might even make it into the family album.

On the Social Studies TAAS, you'll see a fair number of straightforward questions, like, "Who wrote the Declaration of Independence?" that test your knowledge of historical facts. How well you do on these questions will depend primarily on how much history you know. In other words, do you have a 16-piece knowledge of history or a 128-piece knowledge of history? Of course, if you know a lot of history, you'll do well, but if you don't, things can get tough—as tough as drawing a rainbow with just 16 colors.

This chapter will help you focus on some of the major historical facts you'll want to study for this test. By bolstering your skills, you should be able to go into the test with a 64-piece box of historical knowledge. Granted, that's only half of the 128-piece box, but 64 pieces is much better than 16 pieces. You goal should be to know enough history to pass the test.

## How the Social Studies Test Adds Up

The Social Studies test consists of 40 multiple-choice questions that test eight TEA Objectives. They are:

| TAAS Objective | Number of Questions on Social Studies TAAS |
|---|:---:|
| 1. Civic Values and Responsibilities | 5 |
| 2. Economic Influences on U.S. History | 5 |
| 3. Political Influences on U.S. History | 5 |
| 4. Geographic Influences on U.S. History | 5 |
| 5. Historical Concepts and Information | 5 |
| 6. Sociological and Cultural Influences on U.S. History | 5 |
| 7. Interpret Social Studies Data | 5 |
| 8. Critical Thinking Skills | 5 |
| **Total Number of Questions** | 40 |
| **Minimum Number of Correct Answers Needed to Pass** | 32 |

The Social Studies test is similar to the other subject tests in several ways.

1. As on science, you don't need to know the exact historical (or scientific) fact to get a problem right.

2. As on math and science, there are charts and graphs requiring the same skills.

3. As on the Science TAAS, how you fare on this particular TAAS exam won't affect your advancement to grade 9.

4. POE is still your friend.

The main difference between the Social Studies test and the other subject tests is the fact that here, you'll need to know some basic history. There's no getting around this. You'll recall that for the Science test, you needed a basic knowledge of science, but the fact is that you know more about basic scientific phenomena like sunlight and electricity than you realize. This isn't the case with history—it's quite possible that you have no clue who wrote the Bill of Rights—and no amount of everyday experience will help you bridge that gap. Therefore, you've got to get a good grasp on the fundamentals, and then you can use Elimination to get the right answer. For instance, look at the following question.

1. In the sixteenth century, one effect of European contact with the Americas was

   A. a rich flowering of trade between Spain and the ancient Mayan civilization.

   B. widespread slaughter of North American buffalo by European settlers.

   C. a surge in Native American populations.

   D. a huge influx of wealth into Europe from the New World.

Whether or not you can use POE on question 1 will be a function of what you know about the first Europeans and the New World. The diseases carried by Christopher Columbus and others wiped out millions of Native Americans, so C is wildly wrong. B, widespread slaughter of buffalo, was done by Americans much later than the sixteenth century, so that leaves A or D. Either take a guess at this point or remember that the Spanish and others took tons of gold from the New World, primarily through plunder. The answer is D.

## The Moderately Sized Three Question Types—Social Studies Style

### 1. Visual Information Questions

There are lots of pictures on the Social Studies test, though not quite as many as on the Science test. You can expect to see about 5 questions with maps, 6–10 questions that use charts, and a variety of questions with graphs, diagrams, and other visual bric-a-brac. Again, a chart question is solved just like any other chart question you've seen. A map question could look something like this:

2. The shaded portion of the map above shows the
   A. Northwest Territory.
   B. Louisiana Purchase.
   C. Gadsden Purchase.
   D. Oregon Territory

Geography alone won't get you the answer here; you'll need to know some U.S. history. You could also use POE and guess. If you know where Louisiana and Oregon are, you can rule out B and D, since neither one is near the shaded area. That leaves A and C, and since the shaded area isn't in the northwest portion of the United States, a better guess is C. The Gadsden Purchase took place in 1853, when Mexico sold a portion of southern Arizona and New Mexico to the United States.

### 2. Mini-Reading Passage Questions

For these questions, you'll have to answer questions that follow a 50–200 word passage. The questions might look difficult at first, and because they require a bit of time to read, it's a good idea to save them for your second pass. Just remember to refer to the passage for your answers.

## Strategy

On Mini-Reading Passage questions, review the question(s) before you begin to read You'll get an idea beforehand of what to look for.

Use the speakers' statements and your knowledge of history to answer the following question.

Speaker 1: People in Western Europe were persecuting my family and me because of our religion, so we took a boat and came to the New World. We eventually settled in the St. Lawrence River area.

Speaker 2: In search of glory along the frontier, I saw an ad in the paper that talked about a colony that Stephen Austin was starting on Mexican territory. I left Virginia to move there.

Speaker 3: When gold was discovered at Sutter's Mill, I left my home in the Appalachians and went to find my fortune.

Speaker 4: A glass merchant by trade, I left Germany for the New World. Since my glassware was fairly expensive, I decided to set up shop in one of the larger metropolitan centers along the East Coast.

3. Speaker 2 settled in which location?
   A. California

   B. New York

   C. Quebec

   D. Texas

This question illustrates why reading a question beforehand is a good idea. Once you do, you'll realize that you have to read only Speaker 2, since the question concerns only him. The rest of the speakers are there merely to provide incorrect answer choices, and to take up your time reading all that information.

What's the correct answer? It's D, and there are two ways to reach this answer:

1. The "Austin" in "Stephen Austin" made you think Texas; or

2. You remembered that the TAAS is the Texas Assessment of Academic Skills, so you picked D, Texas. Overall, this isn't a bad strategy. Texas-based history and geography will predominate on this test, so if you have to make an educated guess, pick Texas-related answers over those identifying other areas of the country.

### 3. Historical Questions

While the answers to some questions can be found right in the accompanying passage or illustration, for other questions you'll have to know the historical facts being discussed. These questions cover a broad range of topics, but the TEA does have some favorites.

**Social Studies TAAS Favorites**

1. **The Civil War/Slavery.** Since the Civil War tore the United States in half, it's a topic that often comes up. Slavery, being the predominant cause of the war, is also a hot topic. Make sure you understand the big picture about both of these events. You don't need to know the chronological order of every skirmish in the Civil War, but you do need to be able to answer such basic questions as:

    1. Who fought on which sides? What were the opposing sides called?

    2. What were the causes of the war?

    3. What years did the war occur?

4. Who were the political leaders of the countries involved?

5. When and how did it war end?

6. What were the major battles/events?

7. What were some of the social side effects after the war?

8. Who won?

2. **Expansion into the West/the Railroad.** These questions probe your knowledge about the effects of building the transcontinental railroad. Since many towns in Texas are named after railroad bigwigs, such as Giddings, this topic should be easy to research.

3. **Bill of Rights.** TAAS Objective Civic Values and Responsibilities often asks questions relating to the Bill of Rights, especially free speech.

4. **Founding Fathers.** People like Thomas Jefferson and Thomas Paine sometimes make an appearance in the Social Studies TAAS. Brush up on your America: The Early Years facts.

Learning these facts, combined with your knowledge of charts and reading passage skills, should be enough to get you a decent score on this exam. You should be able to approach each question and have a good chance of solving it. Just remember that the correct answer will always be there, waiting for you like the pot of gold at the end of a nicely drawn rainbow.

# Chapter 8

# RESULTS

## HOW YOUR GRADE 8 TAAS SCORES ARE EXACTLY LIKE YOUR GRADE 7 TAAS SCORES

At last, a chapter title that speaks for itself. If you remember how the TAAS is scored from your grade 7 results, then you'll already know the bulk of this chapter. However, if you wiped all of that information from your mind as soon after that test as possible, you might want this refresher.

Your scores will be broken down into three categories: a raw score, a raw subscore, and the Texas Learning Index. The *raw score*, which is the one you'll be most interested in, shows how many questions you got right on each subject test. For instance, if you get a $\frac{48}{60}$ on the Math TAAS, it means you answered 48 out of 60 questions correctly. Since 40 out of 60 is the minimum passing score, this means you passed. Hooray!

**Internet Information:** For the most recent information about the TAAS, check out the TEA Web site at http://www.tea.state.tx.us/student.assessment.

The *raw subscore* shows how well you did on the TAAS Objectives in each section. To return to the $\frac{48}{60}$ example, there would be a breakdown of how you did on each Math Objective. A $\frac{3}{4}$ on Number Concepts (Objective 1) would mean that you got 3 out of 4 questions right. Teachers often use this breakdown to examine students' areas of weakness.

If you meet the minimum passing score on all TAAS Objectives for a subject, you'll also receive a "Mastering All Objectives" notification. Anyone who *Masters All Objectives* definitely passes that subject test. However, you don't need to master *all* the objectives to pass. In other words, you could miss all four questions in Number Concepts (Objective 1), but then do really well on Objectives 11–13. The fact that you did poorly on one concept would be made up by doing well on the others.

The *Texas Learning Index* (TLI) is a scaled score given on both the Math and Reading sections. The TLI is generally between 0 and 100, and any score over 70 means you passed the section. Of course, if you answered fewer than 40 of the 60 math questions, then your TLI would be under 70. In other words, you can't fail in your raw score, and then go on to receive a passing TLI score.

In terms of how the TAAS is scored, this is the end of the story. But *end of the story* in this instance only means *end of the discussion on how you scored on one standardized test.* This test should be seen for what it is—an interesting checkpoint along a very long highway. Some students who score at the lowest level on this test will go on to graduate from prestigious universities with advanced degrees, while others who score at the highest level will struggle to finish high school. Your scores simply highlight the areas in which you need improvement. So regardless of how you do, try not to lose confidence in yourself or doubt your ability to succeed. Of all the advice given in this book, nothing is more important—or more accurate—than that.